Games, Information, and Politics

Analytical Perspectives on Politics

Political Science is developing rapidly and changing markedly. Keeping in touch with new ideas across the discipline is a challenge for political scientists and for their students.

To help meet this challenge, the series Analytical Perspectives on Politics presents creative and sophisticated syntheses of major areas of research in the fields of political science. In each book, a high-caliber author provides a clear and discriminating description of the current state of the art and a strong-minded prescription and structure for future work in the field.

These distinctive books provide a compact review for political scientists, a helpful introduction for graduate students, and central reading for advanced undergraduate courses.

Games, Information, and Politics

Applying Game Theoretic Models
to Political Science

Scott Gates and Brian D. Humes

Ann Arbor

THE UNIVERSITY OF MICHIGAN PRESS

Copyright © by the University of Michigan 1997
All rights reserved
Published in the United States of America by
The University of Michigan Press
Manufactured in the United States of America
⊗ Printed on acid-free paper

2000   1999   1998   1997   4   3   2   1

A CIP catalog record for this book is available from the British Lιu. ary.

Library of Congress Cataloging-in-Publication Data

Gates, Scott.
    Games, information, and politics : applying game theoretic models
to political science / Scott Gates and Brian D. Humes.
        p.   cm. — (Analytical perspectives on politics)
    Includes bibliographical references and index.
    ISBN 0-472-09564-1 (cloth). — ISBN 0-472-06564-5 (paper)
    1. Game theory.   2. Political science—Mathematical models.
I. Humes, Brian D.   II. Title.   III. Series.
JA72.5.G37   1996
320'.01'51—dc20   96-35062
                                                        CIP

To my parents, from Scott
and
To my family, Evelyn, Nathaniel, and Maggie, from Brian

Contents

Preface

We wrote this book for those political scientists who have an interest in game theory and want to know more. Most political scientists now know some rudimentary game theory but really do not understand how it can be used to improve our understanding of politics. Our intention is to address this problem. In other words, we aim to demonstrate to scholars who have little or no training in formal theory how game theoretic analysis can be applied to politics. We provide applications of game theoretic models to three subfields of political science—American government and politics, comparative politics, and international relations. But more significantly we demonstrate how game theory can be substantively applied to each of these subfields by drawing from three distinct pieces of research. While this book introduces many concepts, it is not a text in game theory (although it certainly could be used in association with one). What we really want to do here is clear up some common misperceptions about game theory and show how it can be used to improve our understanding of politics.

This book originated with a series of conversations regarding the state of game theory in political science. Our conversation basically went as follows: game theory has been a part of political science since the end of World War II. But surprisingly, despite this long shared history, the influence of and appreciation for game theory have been uneven. We concluded that this issue needed to be addressed. What began as a series of gripe sessions evolved into a paper. With the encouragement of Colin Day at the University of Michigan Press, the paper became the basis of this book.

Many people helped us improve this manuscript. Becky Morton and David Leblang used our manuscript in their courses and provided extremely valuable comments. Evelyn Fink and Ken Williams also read several drafts; their criticisms proved to be invaluable. Jon Hovi, Gretchen Hower, and Bjørn Erik Rasch helped us enormously with their insightful comments. David Rohde and an anonymous reviewer for the *American Journal of Political Science* made very useful comments on our paper, which eventually evolved into this book. The ANZUS example that serves as a basis of chapter 2 was initially part of a collaborative effort between James Alt, Randall Calvert, and Brian Humes. John Aldrich was instrumental in the development of chapter 3. Sherry Bennett Quiñones's earlier collaboration with Scott was instrumental in the development of the introduction and chapter 4. Misha Taylor's comments on chapter 5 were also quite valuable. We also extend our thanks to Colin Day, who started us along, Malcolm Litchfield and Charles Myers, who helped us finish, the editors of the series on Analytical Perspectives on Politics, and several anonymous reviewers of our proposal and manuscript at the University of Michigan Press.

Our graduate students at Michigan State University, the University of Trondheim, and the University of Nebraska who served as guinea pigs as we used the manuscript in our game theory courses also deserve our thanks. Scott extends special appreciation to Renee Agress, Chris Butler, Lu-Huei Chen, Erick Duchesne, Sara McLaughlin, Pål Martinussen, Anette Einarsen, Ståle Tømmerrås, Pål Bakken, Tina Vikhagen, Marit Masdal, Chris Sprecher, Bryan Marshall, and Junhan Lee. Brian especially thanks Kelly Kate Pease, Jeff Walz, Cameron Thies, Ethan Zorich, Linda Swanson, Albert van Cleef, Dan Cox, Debra Bozell, Scott Brunner, and Michele Leonard for their comments on the manuscript and its precursors.

Scott sends special thanks to Ola Listhaug, who provided a wonderful environment for finishing the manuscript at the University of Trondheim in Norway.

In addition, we would like to thank those individuals who helped introduce us to game theory. None of these individuals should be held responsible for any mistakes that might be found in this book. They should take credit for anything that is correct in the following pages. Scott would like to thank his friend Doug Dion, who sparked an interest in game theory through the years both at the University of Minnesota's Department of Applied and Agricultural Economics and at the Department of Political Science at the University of Michigan. Brian would like to thank Kenneth Shepsle, Randall Calvert, John Roberts, David Kreps, and Robert Wilson. He would also especially like to thank Forrest Nelson and Chong Lim Kim, who first interested him in game theory.

CHAPTER 1

Modeling with Games

A *game* involves situations in which individuals are aware that their actions affect one another. To study the strategic interaction of individuals, we use game theory. Social, political, and economic interactions abound with such strategic behavior. Politics, in particular, is inherently strategic. All aspects of politics are affected by it. International relations, for example, is rife with strategic interaction, be it military or economic. Parties in a legislature or parliament regularly engage in strategic intrigue as they attempt to outmaneuver the opposition. Individual politicians must attend to strategy or their careers will be amazingly brief.

Given the central role strategic interaction plays in politics, it is hardly surprising that so many have applied game theory to the study of politics. Game theoretic analysis has played a significant role in the study of political science for more than 40 years. In fact, these models have been applied to international conflict and strategic studies for almost as long as the field of game theory has existed.[1] Game theory subsequently has been employed to research in all the subfields of political science. As expected, game theoretic applications to political science have followed the same path as those of game theory in general. The intellectual history of game theory is marked by several innovations that have revolutionized the field.[2]

John von Neumann derived the first prominent game theoretic

---

1. Some of the earliest applications were seen at the RAND Corporation, where a number of prominent game theorists gathered to apply game theory to military and strategic policy. Even Pete Seeger sang about the game theorists at RAND: "The RAND Corporation's the boon to the world / They think all day long for a fee. / They sit and play games about going up in flames / For counters they use you and me. . . ." ("The RAND Hymn," words by Malvina Reynolds, copyright 1961 Schroder Music Co., ASCAP, renewed in 1989 by Nancy Schimmel [cited in Poundstone 1992, 83]). Some of the game theorists working at RAND in the 1940s and 1950s included the following: John Von Neumann (the inventor of game theory), Kenneth Arrow, George Dantzig, Melvin Dreshler, Daniel Ellsberg (yes, the one of Pentagon Papers fame), R. Duncan Luce, John Nash, Anatol Rappoport, Lloyd Shapley, and Martin Shubik (Poundstone 1992, 94).

2. Readers interested in a more complete history of game theory should read Aumann (1989).

result with the Minimax Theorem in 1928.[3] Game theory, however, was familiar only to mathematicians until von Neumann together with Oskar Morgenstern wrote *Theory of Games and Economic Behavior* (1944). All game theory applied to economics and political science can be traced back to this work. For political scientists, an equally important book in this area is Luce and Raiffa's *Games and Decisions* (1957). This text served as the basis for most courses on game theory at the graduate level in political science until the early 1980s (Riker 1990, 14–15).

Both books prominently featured zero-sum and cooperative games. Zero-sum games model situations in which one person's gain is equal to another's loss. For example, most sports competitions are zero sum in that one player or team earns a win and the other a loss. From von Neumann and Morgenstern's discussion of zero-sum games came many features of modern game theory (such as mixed strategies), but for the most part zero-sum games have little application to political science.[4] Riker notes that theoreticians at the Rand Corporation focused on zero-sum games because of their focus on the winning or losing of battles. Political scientists, however, were interested in larger events in which one actor's gains do not exactly equal the other actor's losses (Riker 1990, 15). In fact, Brams's use of zero-sum games in the *The Presidential Election Game* (1978) is one of the few uses of this type of game in political science.

Today in political science noncooperative game theory is applied much more often than is cooperative game theory, but there was a time when cooperative game theory played a dominant role. The fundamental assumption underlying cooperative games is that binding contracts are possible; this leads to an analytical focus on how a number of players divide a joint product. The Shapley value is one of the first applications of cooperative games to politics. In fact, Shapley and Shubik (1954) was the first article to discuss game theory in a political science journal. Shapley's power index has been applied to a number of political situations. The first application by Shapley and Shubik (1954) involved measuring power in legislative committees. Other applications include Mann and Shapley (1964) on the relative powers of states in the electoral college, Riker and Shapley's analysis (1968) of weighted voting systems, Brams and Riker (1972) on the

---

3. Some authors also point to Emilé Borel's work, which mathematically defined pure and mixed strategies in the early 1920s.

4. Almost all games applied to politics are non–zero-sum games wherein one player's gain does not necessarily equal another's loss. In non–zero-sum games some outcomes involve both players benefiting.

bandwagon effect in coalition formation, and Ordeshook and Riker's examination (1973) of changing rules in the Security Council of the United Nations. Few political scientists have used the Shapley value since the development of the Banzhaf index (1965) and Straffin's critique (1977) of the Shapley index.

Cooperative bargaining and coalition games have also had a rich history in political science. Such works were applied to the study of legislatures, parliaments, committees, and international alliances. For example, Riker's *Theory of Political Coalitions* (1963) used von Neumann and Morgenstern's model of cooperative N-person games to derive the size principle.[5] Riker applied the size principle to international alliances and political parties in the United States. Most of the other works using this notion examined the size of cabinet governments in parliamentary systems. These include Leiserson (1968), Axelrod (1970), DeSwaan (1970), Taylor and Laver (1973), Browne and Franklin (1973), Dodd (1976), and Schofield and Laver (1985). While there is a long history of cooperative games applied to political science, noncooperative games predominate.[6] For example, one of the few recent applications of cooperative game theory is in the international realm (Ordeshook and Niou 1989a, 1989b).[7] One of the major reasons for the downfall of cooperative games is that this type of game assumes that binding agreements are possible. This assumption has fallen into disfavor with a number of political scientists. Because cooperative game theory is no longer used by many political scientists (and is used by a decreasing number of economists), we do not discuss cooperative games in this book.

Noncooperative games make no allowance for binding commitments. Such games provide the basic approach for most of political science today. John Nash revolutionized game theory with the development of noncooperative games.[8] The conceptual device that spurred the development of noncooperative games was the Nash equilibria. While we devote more attention to this concept in chapter 2, Nash equilibria are defined as a combination of strategies whereby no player has an incentive to unilaterally alter her or his own strategy. All noncooperative game theory today rests on Nash's work from the 1950s.

---

5. Riker's size principle is defined as follows: in constant sum and zero-sum cooperative N-person games with transferable utility, only minimum winning coalitions form.

6. For more discussion, see reviews by Wagner (1983) and Snidal (1985).

7. Ordeshook and Niou 1989a is a cooperative model, while the 1989b paper is a noncooperative version of the model of balance of power.

8. John Nash won the Nobel Prize in economics in 1994, along with Reinhard Selten and John Harsanyi, whose work we describe subsequently.

The best known noncooperative game is the Prisoners' Dilemma. Many scholars have used this simple two-person non–zero-sum game to analyze many forms of political interaction. For example, Rappoport and Chammah (1965) applied this model directly to international politics. Many others have applied this model to other arenas. In the late 1970s another application of the Prisoners' Dilemma model had a significant impact on political science as well as population biology. This application involved the analysis of repeated Prisoners' Dilemma games as was done by Axelrod (1981, 1984) and Maynard-Smith (1982). This analysis led to a huge growth of applications of game theory in both of these fields. Axelrod and Dion (1988) and Axelrod and D'Ambrosio (1994) provide exhaustive listings of the uses of this work in political science and biology.

While many political scientists applied simple two-person non–zero-sum games to political situations with the aide of Nash equilibria, Reinhard Selten (1965) refined this concept with the development of the concept of subgame perfect equilibria. While we discuss subgame perfect equilibria in greater detail in chapters 2 and 4, it suffices to say here that this concept involves players looking forward through the steps of a game and that all players follow through the play of the game making consistently rational decisions. This concept rules out some Nash equilibria that seem unreasonable.

John Harsanyi (1967) introduced the concept of incomplete information to game theory in the late 1960s. Chapters 2, 5, and 6 focus on the role information plays in a game. For now, we will define incomplete information as a player being uncertain of the other player's payoffs. Instead of knowing the other player's payoffs with certainty, the first player believes that the second could have one of many sets of payoffs. To make the analysis tractable, we assume that the first player can assign a probability to each set of payoffs.

The equilibrium concepts of perfect Bayesian and sequential equilibrium serve a central role in most prominent works in political science today.[9] Through the use of the concept of perfect Bayesian equilibria, Harsanyi was able to model how players update their beliefs about another player as a game progresses. We demonstrate applications of this concept in chapters 5 and 6.

For political science these equilibria concepts allow us to model situations involving uncertainty. For example, see Calvert (1986) for a review of models of uncertainty in politics and Banks (1991) for a

---

9. A number of game theorists have further refined the equilibria concept. Examples include trembling hand perfect, divine, proper, evolutionary stable strategy, intuitive and reactive equilibria, and many more. Discussion of these concepts is beyond the scope of this book.

discussion of signaling games in political science. In electoral politics, incomplete information models have been applied to a number of topics: why people vote (Palfrey and Rosenthal 1985), candidate competition and voting behavior (McKelvey and Ordeshook 1986), retrospective voting (Ferejohn 1986; Austen-Smith and Banks 1989), the effect of voting rules (Myerson and Weber 1993), popular initiatives (Lupia 1992), and political activism (Lohmann 1993). To model political control of bureaucracy, a number of authors have also employed incomplete information models (Bendor, Taylor, and Van Gaalen 1987; Banks 1989; Banks and Weingast 1992). Leadership is examined by Calvert (1987) among legislators, by Alt, Calvert, and Humes (1988) in an international context, and by Bianco and Bates (1990) in a more general setting. In international relations, models of uncertainty examine issues of deterrence and crisis bargaining (Morrow 1989; Powell 1990; Kilgour and Zagare 1991; Bueno de Mesquita and Lalman 1992; Fearon 1994), arms control agreements (Wittman 1989; Downs and Rocke 1990; Kilgour and Brams 1992), domestic-international two-level games (Mo 1994), and alliance formation (Morrow 1994). This is just a small sample of the many many applications to political science.

Despite the long history shared by game theory and political science, many political scientists remain unaware of the many exciting game theoretic techniques that have been developed over the years. Because they are unaware of these developments, many scholars continue to use inappropriate techniques to examine political situations. As a result, they use overly simple games to illustrate more complicated processes. The problem is model underspecification. These authors often overextend their simple models, leaving many important factors discussed in the text but not incorporated into the model itself. Such works often discuss, but do not model, such features as bluffing, reputation, commitment, and other factors brought about by uncertainty. Techniques explicitly modeling uncertainty, asymmetric information, and commitment allow game theoretic models to directly address these more complex political interactions. Our intention in writing this book is to introduce some of these modeling techniques to a diverse set of political scientists. This book is about applying game theoretic models to political science.

The Advantages of Game Theoretic Modeling

Why use game theoretic models? Beyond the advantages achieved from any form of social science modeling, formal analyses, such as game theory, are characterized by rigor and precision. So what do we gain from rigor and precision? First and foremost, formal analysis requires that the modeler make the assumptions explicit. Verbal arguments, in contrast, often possess hidden or blurred assumptions. One of the central tasks of formal modeling is to lay out the assumptions explicitly. This focus on assumptions sheds additional light on the connections between the broad theory and model we are developing to study a particular social phenomenon. The second advantage from formal modeling stems from analytical clarity and rigor. Arguments structured by formal logic or mathematical analysis are explicit and unambiguous. Such models demand that the links between assumptions and analysis are clear. Moreover, formal analysis allows us to eliminate certain conclusions that contradict the assumptions of a model. In this way formal models can be used to determine inconsistencies in analysis or disjunctures between assumptions and conclusions. There is no room for whitewashing the details. Formal modeling requires a precision that rewards the investigator with clear insight, consistency of argument, and explicit reasoning.

Game theory as applied in political science belongs solidly in the camp of social scientific research. This becomes quite evident when we relate game theoretic modeling to King, Keohane, and Verba's (1994) four characteristics of scientific research.

1. *The goal is inference.* Formal analysis in general and game theoretic models in particular can provide valuable insight. The deductive logic employed by these techniques aims at providing an explanation of various aspects of social interaction. This is not a simple reporting of facts and opinion but a carefully laid out and developed formal argument. Deductive analysis works from general principles to specific inferences. Developing a formal model forces one to think through underlying assumptions and the logical structure of an argument. It is this rigor and explicitness of game theoretic analysis that can give us insight into various social interactions.

2. *The procedures are public.* The rigor of formal analysis and the explicit presentation of assumptions make this an especially public enterprise. The logic of the analysis is presented for all to see and evaluate. With formal models there is no glossing over the details. This explicit presentation aids in the accumulation of knowledge as others are able to clearly build on previous work.

3. *The conclusions are uncertain.* Formal models, and more particularly game theoretic models, are especially effective in

providing unexpected results. Such unexpected results are clearly uncertain. The logical structure of these models sometimes produces conclusions that are at variance with accepted wisdom. In fact, the formal structure of these arguments can serve to demonstrate inconsistencies in the reasoning that was used to arrive at the accepted wisdom. Formal models can also be used to show how commonly used tests of theories are inappropriate. In this way we see how the formal structure of a game theoretic model often forces us to challenge conventional wisdom that is less formally grounded.

4. *The content is the method.* The validity of a scientific argument depends on a set of rules of inference. Game theoretic modeling is characterized by a set of explicit rules regarding the procedure by which a social phenomenon is analyzed. This book focuses on this method. Our book is about applying game theoretic models specifically to political interactions between individuals.

The basic orientation of game theoretic modeling is toward the development of general explanations. This involves the development of theory. The enterprise is not to take a particular case, design a game in which the payoffs lead to the outcome that actually occurred, and then claim that the case is now explained. Along these lines, "too many 'applications' of game theory have merely been in the spirit of sorting out whether the Cuban Missile Crisis was really Chicken or Prisoners' Dilemma."[10] Such an approach ends up fitting the structure of some preexisting game theoretic model to a particular situation, but it does not generate new explanations or predictions. Such an approach toward game theory fails to meet the criteria of good social science.

The principal advantage of formal modeling is the clarity and rigor afforded through deductive analysis. For game theoretic analysis this means identifying equilibrium conditions not predicting specific outcomes of a particular case. By focusing on equilibria, a modeler is developing hypotheses about how the world works. Yet the rigor of game theory cries out for application where strategic interactions are to be explained. Of course, one hopes that the inference gained from game theoretic modeling will be used by others to help explore specific situations of strategic interaction, for otherwise the game theory has little to offer the scientific community. Our concern is that all too

---

10. See Snidal (1985, 26–27) for criticism of such applications of game theory.

often the application of specific game theoretic insights is mistaken (as well as misused) for the much broader goal of developing general models. Like any other abstract model, game theory helps identify relevant information, relevant processes, and likely outcomes. If a butcher shop's sales were down one particular month, the butcher would no more blame comparative statics results for the lack of sales than she would blame the sun, moon, and stars. But she might use the ideas from comparative statics to examine how her price structure compares to those of other markets. Yet it may not explain everything. They may have just started construction on the street in front of her store.

This is a common occurrence in the literature, where researchers applying game theory (unfortunately in too simplistic a manner) often express dismay that the theory does not perfectly explain their particular situation. When they do so, first, they are judging it by a unrealistic standard, and, second, they are ignoring the difference between game theoretic modeling and its application.

As with other social science models, game theoretic models do not even attempt to address all the complexity of social interaction. The value of modeling comes through the development of an elegant explanation. For game theory this means narrowing down the context of a social interaction. Only the essentially relevant actors and choices are considered; additional assumptions can be considered as the model is developed. The objective should be to provide the best explanation with the simplest model. In this respect game theory is no different from other social science approaches.

The Basic Assumptions of Game Theory

Game theoretic modeling constitutes one type of rational choice theory. When we speak of rationality we refer to some form of goal-directed behavior. As such this means that individuals are seen to choose the means to best gain a set of ends, where goals are related to outcomes through action or choice. More formally we make three basic assumptions about individual's preferences: *completeness*, *fixed preferences*, and *transitivity*. Completeness means that actors prefer one outcome over another or they are indifferent. Essentially this entails some notion of comparison and choice over alternative outcomes. Fixed preferences assumes that an actor's preferences over a set of outcomes do not change. Actors may alter the means of achieving these outcomes (changing strategies or actions), but they do not change their basic underlying preferences over the consequences. Transitivity, whereby an individual preferring A to B and B to C will then prefer *A* to *C*, precludes preference cycles. For example, an individual preferring strawberry ice cream to vanilla and preferring vanilla to chocolate operating under transitivity will then prefer strawberry to chocolate. This implies some coherence and consistency in choice. These three assumptions serve as the basis for the conceptualization of preferences. The concept of utility, in turn, serves as a way of measuring preferences. One can also characterize the assumption of rationality as the assumption of utility maximization. The three assumptions of rational choice characterize what is meant by rational choice. Fundamentally a rational actor possesses preferences over a set of outcomes and, in turn, selects actions that satisfy these preferences. This is the essence of choice in game theory.

Game theory as a way to model strategic interaction relies on these assumptions of rational choice. Players of a game are seen to make a choice based on the assumptions of rational choice while taking into account the choices of other players. Game theory is akin to decision theory except for this latter point. Players want to make the best choice for themselves, but they realize that obtaining their best choice is only partially dependent on their own actions. They must take into account the influence of other people's choices.

Game theoretic models also typically assume that players of a game possess *common knowledge*. By this we assume that everybody in a game knows something, everyone knows that everybody knows it, everybody knows that everyone knows that everybody knows something, and so on, ad infinitum. Common knowledge plays a fundamental role in the manner in which players' expectations take shape. It is a beginning point for modeling the strategic interest that is the essence of game theory. Game theorists typically assume that players possess common knowledge[11] about the rationality of other players and the structure of the game and other players' preferences. In other words, we assume that individuals are characterized by the common knowledge that other players are rational actors, as they are themselves. It is also assumed that players possess common knowledge about the rules of the game that they are playing.[12]

How do individuals playing a game select an action? Game theo-

---

11. For a thorough discussion of the topic of common knowledge, see Geanakoplos 1992, 1994.

12. Common knowledge is exhibited in (1) cases where it is common knowledge both that the horizon is infinite and what the number of stages is, (2) cases where it is common knowledge that the horizon is infinite, and (3) cases where it is common knowledge that the horizon is finite but the number of stages is uncertain. In fact, this case can be broken down into two categories—one where the maximum number of iterations is common knowledge and one where this number is unknown. The former category can be shown to reflect the finite horizon case. The second category is more similar to the infinite horizon case.

rists answer this question by focusing on two aspects of behavior: rational choice and strategic interaction. Rational choice provides a way of understanding an individual's preference for one outcome over another. Strategic interaction then shapes the action that is selected since it is the interaction of choice that leads to different outcomes associated with different payoffs. Game theoretic models then explain the structure and rules for how individuals' decisions and actions are interrelated and how different social outcomes come to be.

Applying Game Theory to Politics

The goal of social science is to explain, predict, and understand human behavior. As such, it is not so much the goals of different methodological techniques within the social sciences that differ but rather the orientations of each. Game theoretic analysis fundamentally focuses on particular aspects of a social interaction. Such formal models allow us to form clear and explicit assumptions and examine their implications through formal analysis. We learn about social behavior through the cumulative knowledge gained by the analysis of such models. In other words, accumulation of knowledge takes place by seeing how different assumptions lead to different predictions or explanations. In such a way, game theoretic models provide a progressive understanding of the world. Those who set out to directly "test" game theoretic models miss the point. Green and Shapiro (1994) make this mistake in examining the fruits of rational choice modeling.

The problems of model misspecification and underspecification must be addressed by any social science method. Game theoretic modelers need to attend to these problems, as does anyone who employs statistical analysis. Specification problems mean that a model fails to incorporate significant aspects of the phenomenon being analyzed. In the case of misspecification, the model involves the incorporation of the wrong elements into a model. For the problem of model underspecification there are elements missing from the model. These two problems are evident in many attempts by political scientists to apply game theoretic models to their subject matter.

These problems are manifested in three common ways when game theory is applied to politics. These are: not explicitly modeling the structure of decisions and actions, not explicitly modeling information asymmetries that may exist between political actors playing a game, and not taking into account the strategic interaction between players. These three errors amount to problems of model misspecification and underspecification. Such problems can be avoided to a large degree by using game theoretic models as they should be used, as rigorous deductive analytical tools. We can address problems of model underspecification and misspecification by employing some of the many techniques that have been developed over the last few decades in game theory. One way to avoid such problems is to focus on the enterprise of model building.

Social scientific modeling relies on three basic stages of model building: conceptualization, operationalization, and interpretation. We examine each of these stages and discuss how they relate to game theoretic modeling.[13]

Conceptualization and Game Theoretic Modeling

Conceptualization involves specification. In game theoretic analysis, conceptualization involves the deduction of the formal game structure. A game includes: the players, the structure of the payoffs, assignment of decision nodes to players, actions, information sets, and probability distributions for each node. In the next chapter we discuss each of these aspects of a game in greater detail.

A game theoretic model has been described as "a special conceptual structure for organizing and structuring thoughts about concepts in an attempt to order them and predict their effects" (Myerson 1992, 62). Formalizing a game, specifying actions, payoffs, information, and so on, imposes restrictions on a model. A game's assumptions constitute the initial conditions within a model and the parameters that will be manipulated. "Rational choice theorists deliberately simplify and abstract reality in their models. Game models do not even attempt to address all the complexity of the social world. Instead, they focus on certain elements of social situations to lay bare how motivations and actions are interrelated" (Morrow 1994, 8). The enterprise of all social science modeling is oriented toward clarification and simplification of complex social interactions, not toward providing a complete picture. Game theoretic modeling is one means of gaining an understanding of specific aspects of different social phenomena.

Operationalization and Game Theoretic Modeling

Operationalization of game theoretic models involves a process of delineating strategies that produce equilibria. After conceptualizing a given theory into a game theoretic form, game theory relies on deduc-

---

13. See Gates and Quinones 1994, wherein the authors compare statistical, empirical, and game theoretic modeling across these stages.

tive analysis of the strategies that produce solutions for the game. These solutions are the equilibria we derive from our games. Chapter 2 devotes considerable attention to the most basic of these concepts, that is, Nash equilibria. Recall that a Nash equilibrium is a situation in which no player has an incentive to unilaterally alter her or his own strategy. In game theoretic models it is assumed that players condition their actions on what they believe is "rational" under certain circumstances.[14] "As in any analytic approach to real-life problems, the best we can hope for is to have a class of models sufficiently rich and flexible that, if anyone objects that our model has neglected some important aspect of the situation that we are trying to analyze, we can generate a more complicated extension of our model that takes this aspect into account" (Myerson 1991, 83).

Operationalization within any modeling framework is a major problem. To a large extent this is unavoidable.[15] How do we translate opaque constructs into tangible variables? Operationalizing constructs into variables within an empirical framework is often problematic; it is often as great an issue for game theoretic models.

Interpretation of Game Theoretic Models

Interpretation of our results is of critical importance. Indeed, this process highlights the real power of game theory, as it is used to generate new findings and understandings of our theories (Snidal 1985). Through the interpretation of our results we develop our explanations and understanding of the real world.[16] The rigorous manner in which game theoretic models are deduced can allow political scientists to evaluate theories in a more rigorous manner.

Examples of Effective Applications of Game Theoretic Models in Political Science

Game theoretic analysis has played a significant role in the field of political science. Over the years we have seen more and more articles using this approach appear in the major journals in the discipline. Many of these are true examples of quality work. Some have led many

---

14. Recall the two central assumptions of game theory: rationality (or utility maximization) and common knowledge.

15. Recall Quine's (1953) critique of the analytic-synthetic distinction.

16. Game theoretic models are rarely explicitly tested with actual observations in the real world. Note, however, some prominent exceptions discussed in the next section. Experiments are the most common empirical approach used to test game theoretic models. See, for example, Morton 1993 (382–392) or Palfrey 1991.

of us to question long-held conventional views. Others serve to confirm certain perspectives. Ultimately, such quality work contributes to the body of knowledge of political science.

We use the following criteria for assessing game theoretic modeling in political science. To a large degree these criteria reflect the qualities of social science research previously discussed. First, such work is characterized by explicit assumptions. Second the analysis is rigorous and clear when the structure of the game (actors, actions, strategies, information, payoffs, and equilibria) are reproducible. Third, the conclusions are clear. These conclusions, in turn, can be used to derive propositions that can be verified empirically. Fourth, the very best of such work forces us to reassess the ways we perceive the world.

High-quality game theoretic work has been applied to all subfields of political science. Nonetheless, it is safe to say that most of it has been used to study voting behavior and legislatures, often (but not always) applied to American government and politics.[17] Our understanding of voting has been greatly influenced by such work as Fiorina (1981); Abramson, Aldrich, and Rohde (1995); Shepsle (1991); and Enelow and Hinich (1984) among others. Similarly the study of legislatures has benefited significantly from the concept of structure-induced equilibrium (Shepsle (1979); Shepsle and Weingast (1987); and Weingast (1989)). Austen-Smith (1990) and Austen-Smith and Riker (1987, 1990) model legislative debate as a signaling game. Baron and Ferejohn (1989) created a cottage industry of game theoretic analyses of the distributional effects of the U.S. Congress's policies. For example, Krehbiel (1991), Kiewiet and McCubbins (1991), and Cox and McCubbins (1993) have all addressed this topic.[18] Applications to parliamentary legislatures have seen the imprint of quality game theoretic work, including that of Dodd (1976), Austen-Smith and Banks (1989, 1990), Laver and Shepsle (1990, 1995), and Baron (1991).

Game theory has also been useful in analyzing international relations. We discuss in subsequent sections several examples of important work in international crisis bargaining. Most of the best work in international relations applies game theory to conflict and general

---

17. We limit our discussion here to noncooperative games.

18. To illustrate the impact of this literature, one needs only to note that both Krehbiel (1991) and Cox and McCubbins (1993) received the Fenno Award from the Legislative Studies Section of the American Political Science Association for the best book published that year in legislative studies. Also, these works have generated a set of articles that consumed two issues of *Legislative Studies Quarterly* and are being published separately in Shepsle and Weingast 1995.

theory. These studies include Niou and Ordeshook (1990) and Powell (1988). There are also some good applications in international political economy, for example, Morrow (1994) and Mo (1994).

Of course, there are many more examples.[19] We only present these few to give an idea of where good work is being applied. For the most part these works possess the qualities of good game theoretic applications in political science. Integrating game theoretic and empirical methods still appears to be a novel idea. A move in this direction can only serve to advance the discipline, as it can help our theories become more rigorous and systematic. If our aim as political scientists is to contribute to the discipline in this manner, then integrating these two analytic disciplines certainly is reaching toward that goal. We now turn to attempts to more explicitly link game theoretic and statistical methods of analysis.

A Deductive Approach to Integration

Game theoretic models can be linked to empirical analysis in a purely deductive manner.[20] The procedure is to take a theory about a particular phenomenon, form a game theoretic model, and subsequently use the game theoretic model to shape an empirical test. This process consists of using game theoretic models a priori as a theoretical device to specify relevant parameters in a model.

One of the first applications of game theory to the study of political science in this manner was Dodd (1976). Dodd applied Riker's notion of minimum winning coalitions to examine the sustainability of parliamentary coalitions in Western Europe. After deriving several hypotheses from Riker's model, Dodd tested these hypotheses using empirical data on the stability of governments in Western Europe. He found that a "key to durable government is the coalitional status of the cabinet; minimum winning cabinets endure whereas cabinets that deviate from minimum winning status do not" (1976, 234). This occurs whether the cabinet is formed of several parties or one majority party. This result helped to change the focus of the durability

---

19. There are several sources that offer reviews of the literature in various fields. For example, O'Neill (1994) provides a comprehensive review of game theoretic models applied to the study of international conflict. Bendor (1988) provides a review of the use of game theory in the study of bureaucracies. Aldrich (1993) reviews the work on voter turnout. Krehbiel (1988) provides a review of the literature on legislatures. Also there are good reviews of the uses of different types of game theoretic models (Calvert 1986; Banks 1991).

20. Much of the following discussion about how game theoretic and statistical modeling techniques can be integrated is derived from Gates and Quinones 1994.

of governments in parliamentary systems, which up to that time had been on the problems of multiparty governments.

Bueno de Mesquita and Lalman (1992) also illustrate how useful it can be to deductively integrate game theoretic and statistical methods. Their analysis begins with an international interaction game characterized by sequential decisions. Bueno de Mesquita and Lalman's game features the actions of two rival nations and the potential outcomes that result from their strategic choices. From this game theoretic model they derive a set of propositions, which, in turn, are used to assess two competing theories of international relations: realpolitik, which stresses the role of systemic constraints, and the domestic politics variant, which features both systemic and domestic political constraints. These propositions are analyzed both formally and empirically through statistical analysis. After examining 707 dyadic interactions, the authors conclude that the domestic politics model provides a better explanation of international relations. The analysis is deductive in that it begins with a general model, general propositions are derived, and finally propositions are empirically analyzed. Of course, Bueno de Mesquita and Lalman's analysis is not purely deductive. In fact, no one's research is ever purely deductive or inductive but exhibits general tendencies in one direction or another.

Using the deductive approach, a game theoretic model is developed and formalized from a more general theory to model a social interaction. Assumptions (initial conditions) and equilibria for the game are then identified. From this analysis, a set of propositions are presented and empirically evaluated. The empirical analysis essentially tests propositions derived from the analysis and identification of equilibria. What this suggests is that propositions can be extracted from game models and empirically tested in an effort to confirm or disconfirm the explanatory power of our models. A deductive approach, in this manner, provides a direct path of integration for game theory and empirical methods.

The deductive approach also provides an opportunity to test a variety of propositions derived from a set of formal models. As a variety of formal models provides a better understanding of the nature of specific social interactions, this type of comparative evaluation of propositions derived from a set of formal models contributes even more to our understanding. In fact, such a comparative evaluation of propositions may be one of the best ways to maintain theoretical analytical rigor and provide a more fully specified empirical model that can be statistically evaluated.

The deductive approach also provides an opportunity to test a variety of propositions derived from a set of formal models. A comparative evaluation of a variety of deductively derived propositions may be one of the best ways to attain more fully specified empirical models that can be statistically evaluated. The deductive approach, however, is not the only path for integrating game theoretic and statistical methods. There is also a more inductive approach.

An Inductive Approach

Game theoretic models can also be used to evaluate empirical results and to compare statistical models. Such an approach could be characterized as possessing inductive characteristics. Such an inductive approach consists of using game theoretic models to compare competing empirical models. This approach has been employed very infrequently. It is interesting to note that these two examples of this inductive approach, Fearon (1994) and Morrow (1989), both involve the study of international crisis bargaining. Like Nalebuff (1986), Powell (1990), Fearon (1990), Wagner (1991), Kilgour (1991), and Bueno de Mesquita and Lalman (1992), Fearon (1994) and Morrow (1989) develop different game theoretic models that examine how sequence and information compel actors to select certain actions in a crisis bargaining situation.

Unlike all of these previous game theoretic analyses of international crisis bargaining (except for Bueno de Mesquita and Lalman 1992), Fearon and Morrow subsequently use their respective game theoretic models to assess the viability of several empirical models of crisis bargaining. In this manner, both demonstrate how game theoretic models can be used to develop testable propositions and reexamine empirical studies. These formal models serve "to draw logical links between postulated underlying processes and empirical regularities. By demonstrating what empirical patterns should follow from an assumed process, the formal model serves as a tool to judge evidence" (Morrow 1989, 964).

In light of his game theoretic model, Fearon reanalyzes Huth (1988) using the same data set (Huth and Russett 1988). Morrow, on the other hand, uses his model to reinterpret a larger set of empirical works, though less directly. Both demonstrate how empirical models of crisis behavior are plagued by the joint problems of selection bias and misspecification. Both of these problems stem from the unobservable nature of beliefs. Fearon presents a model wherein two nations engage each other in a sequential game of threats and action; Morrow develops a sequential equilibrium of the model that characterizes the offers and acceptance of offers for both sides, for all moves within the game theoretic model. From these game theoretic analyses, they evaluate existing empirical models in an attempt to see which studies more appropriately characterize the nature of crises bargaining.

By viewing several empirical studies through the lens of a sequential game, the problems affecting existing empirical models can be more easily detected. As a result, such problems can be corrected so that new conclusions can be drawn. Indeed, this process highlights the real power of game theory, using it to generate new findings and understandings of our theories (Snidal 1985). Moreover, this emphasizes the benefits to be gained from integrating game theory and statistical methods, namely, that competing empirical models can be evaluated for analytic correctness and rigor with a corresponding game theoretic analysis. The game's analytic framework can be used to show systematically which factors are important in explaining behavior and which are improperly being ignored. For example, Fowler (1993) notes that the empirical models of candidate recruitment and the incumbency effect disagree and conflict with each other. Game theory could provide a way to choose between these competing models. Statistical methods are not perfect in choosing between models. Instead, we can use game theory to develop prior knowledge, which would lead us to accept or reject certain statistical results.

This type of formal integration can also be useful for conducting encompassing tests. It has already been established that game theoretic analysis is able to rigorously specify relevant parameters in a model. Moreover, as the previous discussion suggests, it is also able to dismiss parameters that are largely irrelevant in empirical models. As such, if game theoretic analysis is used to assess irrelevant and relevant parameters in empirical models, in the same vein it can be used to determine which models explain more. That is, game theoretic models can help identify and derive empirical models that explain the most and yet at the same time prove to be the most parsimonious. Both inductive and deductive forms of integration can help foster an effective dialogue between these two formal approaches. The combination of the two approaches can help develop systematic and rigorous models in political science.

Our book addresses several problems that are common among game theoretic work applied to political science. Our aim is show how correcting these problems will lead to a better quality of game theoretic modeling.

Overview of Book Chapters

This book features two themes: (1) when is a strategic decision best modeled with game theory and when is it more appropriate to use decision theory? and (2) how should the game be modeled? What are the differences between decision theory and game theory? How can we best model different political situations? In chapter 3 we highlight the differences between these two modeling techniques and comment on their application to politics. In chapter 4 we discuss the conditions under which large N-player games resemble decision theory problems. We further contrast the differences between large N-player and small N-player games. In both of these discussions we to a large extent ask: when is a strategic interaction a game and when is it not? After determining whether game theory is an appropriate modeling tool, we discuss the various game theoretic tools available to the modeler. Our focus here is on the structure of the game. Do the players move simultaneously or sequentially? Do the players possess complete or incomplete information? How does this affect our understanding of a game? How does this affect our understanding of the political concept that we are modeling?

We introduce these methods through the examination of the application of game theory in three subfields of political science. Examining specific uses of game theory in American politics, comparative politics, and international relations, we illustrate how this research can be improved through the application of different methods of game theory. For each example, we focus on what elements have been left out of the model and then address these missing features by developing and applying models that explicitly incorporate these features. Our purpose is not to provide a thorough review of the substantive literature in each of these three cases. The book's orientation is methodological not substantive. Moreover, our focus is not to criticize the examples or their authors; rather, it is to show how these cases can be improved through the use of different methods.

Chapter 2 provides "A Brief Introduction to Game Theoretic Models." Three primary forms of noncooperative game theory have been applied to political science. These three forms consist of simple matrix, repeated, and extensive form games. Of these three, extensive form games have only recently been applied to the study of political situations. The other two forms have been used more frequently. This chapter examines each form in detail and discusses their advantages and disadvantages. The roles of complete and perfect information, incomplete information, and imperfect information games are discussed at length. Different equilibria concepts are also examined in conjunction with the different game forms. We focus primarily on Nash, subgame perfect, and perfect Bayesian equilibrium. Special attention is given to the Folk Theorem in our discussion of repeated games. This chapter introduces the reader to these three principal forms of game theory and provides a basis for the following chapters in which applications using each form are discussed.

This chapter should not be seen as a replacement for a text or course in game theory. Rather, the goal is to introduce the reader to these concepts and their uses. The level of mathematical sophistication is kept at a minimum. After finishing this chapter, the typical reader should have an intuitive understanding of the techniques presented.

Chapter 3 examines "Strategic Choice and Progressive Ambition in American Politics." Rohde (1979) models the choice calculus of members of the U.S. House of Representatives regarding their decision to remain in the House or try for another political office. In this paper, he did not develop a game theoretic model. Instead, he developed a decision theoretic model in which the member makes his or her decision without taking into account the choices of potential competitors. We develop a game theoretic model of this process. This model takes into account other potential entrants. It allows us to illustrate the importance of using game theory instead of decision theory to model strategic interactions and also to review the extensions that were used in the previous two chapters. We focus on when to use decision theory and when to employ game theory.

Chapter 4 is entitled "Dynamic Games and the Politics of International Trade: An Examination of Conybeare's *Trade Wars*." International trade is one of the primary topics of analysis in international political economy. In this chapter, we examine the work of Conybeare (1987), who has applied game theory to study strategic aspects of trade policy. In examining Conybeare's work, we focus on his reliance on simple matrix games. We focus our analysis around three of Conybeare's games applied to the politics of trade wars: Prisoners' Dilemma, Hybrid Chicken–Stag Hunt, and Asymmetric Trade. Expanding on his analysis, we show how topics that he addressed in his analysis but did not explicitly model can be modeled directly. Specifically, we address the topic of game structure through a discussion of simultaneous versus sequential moves. While we demonstrate that both of these types of moves can be considered with simple matrix games, we focus our presentation on the use of extensive form games with imperfect information. We also expand each of his models from two-player games to N-player games. In turn, we highlight the differences between two-player and three-player games and then show the implications of expanding to a large number of players. We end with a model of leadership and international trade that extends several concepts discussed by Conybeare.

Chapter 5 discusses "Information and the Politics of Transitions to Democracy." Democratization, privatization, and other aspects of policy reform attract a good deal of analysis by scholars of comparative politics. Recently, comparativists have begun to apply game theoretic models to their analysis of the strategic aspects of administrative reform. A significant example of such work is Adam Przeworski's study of reform in Latin American and Eastern European democracies (1991). This is an interesting extensive form game-theoretic analysis of the incentives facing politicians who are responsible for initiating reforms.

However, while Przeworski implicitly assumes that there are information asymmetries, he does not explicitly model these asymmetries. By applying a set of models that directly incorporate such conditions as play repeated over time and incomplete information, we show how reputation and credibility can be explicitly incorporated into an analysis of political reform using perfect Bayesian equilibria. We apply this revised model directly to Przeworski's analysis.

Chapter 6, "Commitment, Bluffs, and Reputation," further examines the role of incomplete information in strategic interactions. In this chapter we return to the models developed in chapters 3 and 4 and utilize the modeling techniques introduced in chapter 5. In other words, we present incomplete information models of strategic ambition and asymmetric trade. We also introduce a model of sanctions to highlight the strategic problems of commitment. These models demonstrate the importance of bluffs, commitment, and reputation to political interactions and the advantage of explicitly modeling these concepts.

Game theory and political science share a long history. In recent years this relationship has become even more important. More and more political scientists are utilizing game theoretic models for their analysis. Yet a gap lies between the types of game theoretic models applied to political science and the techniques available. Without knowledge of this new technology, the work in this area tends to overextend simpler game theoretic models. Currently the number of scholars in this field who utilize more sophisticated game theoretic techniques is quite limited. There is a significant need and demand for an introduction and overview of these game theoretic approaches. This book will serve as a vehicle for exposing the political science community to newer game theory technology. This book is designed to be instructive and introductory. Above all we want to demonstrate how game theoretic models should be applied to political science.

CHAPTER 2

A Brief Introduction to Game Theoretic Models

Introduction

In this chapter, a brief overview of game theory is provided. This overview includes examinations of matrix form games, repeated games, extensive form games, and the equilibrium conditions connected with each. The purpose of this chapter is not to provide the reader with an in-depth knowledge of the theory discussed here. Instead, we are providing the reader with an introduction to these concepts that will be used throughout the rest of the book.

In order to present these techniques, we have chosen to motivate our discussions with a substantive example. Specifically, we will focus on the decision by New Zealand to exclude ships with nuclear weapons and the action of the United States to withdraw its support for the ANZUS (Australia, New Zealand, United States) alliance. We use this example because it is easy to understand and can be used to illustrate many different techniques in game theory. The discussion of the disruption of the ANZUS alliance is not meant to be an in-depth case study. Instead, it is used only for the motivation of discussion of the game theory techniques that follow.

This chapter proceeds as follows. First, a brief introduction to the theory of games is provided. Second, a brief discussion concerning the interaction between the United States and New Zealand is presented. Third, a discussion of matrix form games is provided. This discussion, as well as that of other techniques, is motivated with the aid of the ANZUS example. Fourth, we turn to a discussion of extensive form games. Fifth, and finally, a discussion of iterated games is presented.

A Brief Introduction to Game Theory

What is a "game" in game theory? Technically, each game consists of three parts. These are the actors, their strategies, and the payoffs connected with any combination of the players' strategies (Luce and

Raiffa 1957, 5–6).[1] For example, most researchers are familiar with matrix, or strategic form, games. A common game of this type is the Prisoners' Dilemma, which is presented in matrix 1. There are two players in this game: Player 1 and Player 2. These players each have two pure strategies.[2] They may choose either C or D. These strategy combinations are linked to an outcome of the game. For example, if each player chooses C we say that mutual cooperation has occurred. Connected with these outcomes are the payoffs of the game. These payoffs represent how each player values the outcomes of the game. Thus, there are strategies that yield outcomes that yield payoffs for the players of the game. Outcomes and payoffs differ in that payoffs are used to evaluate the outcomes of the game.

In matrix 1 (and throughout this book), Player 1's payoff is listed first and is followed by the payoff to Player 2. Let us examine these payoffs from the perspective of Player 1. Player 1's best payoff occurs when she chooses D and the other player chooses C. With this strategy combination, she receives a payoff of 4. Her next best payoff results when she chooses C and the other player chooses C, which yields a payoff of 3. Her next best payoff occurs when both she and the other player choose D. The payoff connected with this strategy combination is 2. The worst payoff for Player 1 results from the strategy combination $\{C,D\}$ in which the first strategy is that of Player 1 and the second is that of Player 2. This combination yields a payoff of 1. Player 2's payoff structure is similar.

When examining a game, one looks for its equilibrium or equilibria. There are several ways to define an equilibrium in game theory. The most basic of these is a Nash equilibrium. Intuitively, a Nash equilibrium is a set of strategies such that no individual player can be made better off by unilaterally changing his or her choice. There is one Nash equilibrium in the game in matrix 1. This is $\{D,D\}$. To better understand the concept of a Nash equilibrium, we examine this strategy pair more closely in order to investigate why it fits the criteria. In

---

1. This discussion considers only noncooperative game theory. As such, we do not focus on cooperative game theory. This is done for two reasons. First, the topics that are addressed later in the book have traditionally been considered from a noncooperative game theoretic viewpoint. Second, most of the work in political science that uses game theory has used noncooperative game theory. For a good nontechnical introduction to the theory of cooperative games, see Ordeshook 1986 (chap. 7). For applications of cooperative game theory in political science see Ordeshook 1992 (chap. 6).

2. There are actually more than two strategies available to each player. Besides C or D, each player can play a mixed strategy that weights each of these strategies with a nonzero probability. The use of these strategies will be considered more fully later in this chapter as well as in chapter 3.

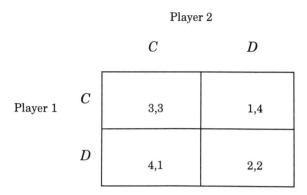

Matrix 1. A matrix game representation of the Prisoners' Dilemma

this strategy pair, Player 1 plays D and Player 2 plays D. For this strategy pair to be an equilibrium, neither player should be willing to unilaterally change his or her strategy. Player 1 has no incentive to change since she receives 2 from playing D and 1 if she chooses C instead. Player 2 also has no reason to change. In his case, D yields a payoff of 2 while C would yield a 1. Thus, $\{D,D\}$ is a Nash equilibrium. The equilibrium of this game is not represented by the outcome associated with the strategies or even with the payoffs associated with this outcome and the strategy combinations that yield it. Rather, it is defined solely by the strategies that yield the payoff.

Another way to think of equilibria in a game is to examine each player's best reply correspondence. This correspondence allows one to consider what a player should do if the other player chooses a certain strategy. For example, if Player 2 chooses D, then Player 1's best reply would be D. Likewise, if Player 2 chooses C, Player 1's best reply would D. Player 1's best reply correspondence when the exogenous variable is Player 2's strategy, then, is

$$R_1(\cdot) = D$$

for all choices by Player 2. Likewise, Player 2's best reply correspondence is:

$$R_2(\cdot) = D$$

for all choices by Player 1. Thus, the strategy combination $\{D,D\}$ is a Nash equilibrium since D is a best reply for both players to each strategy choice of the other player. Once again, the reader should note that the equilibrium of this game is not mutual defection or the payoffs of 2,2. Equilibria are only formed out of strategies.

Another common game is Chicken, which is presented in matrix 2. There are two players in this game: Player 1 and Player 2. These players each have two pure strategies. They may each choose either L or R. Connected with these choices of strategies are the outcomes or payoffs of the game. Let us examine these payoffs from the perspective of Player 1. Player 1's best payoff occurs when she chooses L and Player 2 chooses R. In that case Player 1 gets a payoff of 3. Her next best payoff occurs when she chooses R and Player 2 chooses R. This payoff is a 2. Her third best payoff occurs when she chooses R and Player 2 chooses L, which yields a payoff of 1 for Player 1. Her worst payoff occurs when both players choose L. Player 2 would rank his most preferred outcome to his least preferred outcome in the following manner when the first strategy listed is that of Player 1 and the second is that of Player 2: $\{R,L\}$, $\{R,R\}$, $\{R,L\}$, and $\{L,L\}$.

Remember, a Nash equilibrium is a set of strategies such that no individual player can become better off by unilaterally changing his or her strategy choice. There are three Nash equilibria in this game. Two of these are $\{R,L\}$ and $\{L,R\}$. The other Nash equilibrium in this game is the result of the use of mixed strategies. Mixed strategies result from a player choosing between his or her pure strategies in a random manner. The mixed strategy Nash equilibrium of this game is $\{(0.5,0.5),(0.5,0.5)\}$. With this strategy combination, Player 1 chooses to play R with a probability of 0.5 and to play L with a probability of 0.5. Player 2 chooses between the two strategies with the same probabilities. In order to see why this combination is a Nash equilibrium, we will examine what occurs if Player 1 chooses to change her strategy. We need to calculate Player 1's expected payoff from playing this strategy. The expected payoff of this strategy combination can be calculated in the following manner:

$$EP_1 = 0.5[0.5(0) + 0.5(3)] + 0.5[0.5(1) + 0.5(2)].$$

This yields a payoff of 1.5. If Player 1 chooses one of the pure strategies instead, she would receive one of two payoffs. If she chooses R or L, her payoff would remain at 1.5. Thus, she would be indifferent between playing either of these pure strategies or her mixed strategy if Player 2 continues to play his mixed strategy.

Given this indifference, why is $\{R,(0.5,0.5)\}$ not a Nash equilibrium? It will only be a Nash equilibrium if both players will not unilaterally change strategies. With this combination, Player 2 has an

Player 2

	L	R
L	0,0	3,1
R	1,3	2,2

Player 1 (L, R rows)

Matrix 2. A matrix game representation of Chicken

incentive to change strategies. By moving from (0.5,0.5) to playing L, his payoff changes from 2.5 to 3. Thus, $\{R,(0.5,0.5)\}$ cannot be a Nash equilibrium. Likewise, it can be easily shown that $\{L,(0.5,0.5)\}$ cannot be an equilibrium either.

We have argued that in this game no pure strategy can be combined with the mixed strategy (0.5,0.5) to result in a Nash equilibrium. In fact, $\{(0.5,0.5),(0.5,0.5)\}$ is the only mixed strategy equilibrium in this game. Proving the previous statement is beyond the scope of this chapter.[3] However, we can illustrate what occurs when Player 1 chooses to unilaterally change her strategy. Assume that Player 1 chooses to play (0.7,0.3). Her expected outcome would then become

$$EP_1 = 0.7[0.5(0) + 0.5(3)] + 0.3[0.5(1) + 0.5(2)].$$

The payoff for Player 1 would be 1.5. Player 1 would then be indifferent between playing (0.5,0.5) and (0.7,0.3). However, Player 2 would have an incentive to change strategies. His payoff in this situation would be

$$EP_2 = 0.5[0.7(0) + 0.3(3)] + 0.5[0.7(1) + 0.3(2)].$$

The payoff for Player 2 would then be 1.1, which is less than 1.3, which he would receive if he played R.

The best reply correspondences in this game are more complicated than those for matrix 1. Let α equal the probability that Player 2 plays L. The respective best reply correspondences are

---

3. Moulin (1986, 148–90) provides an excellent introduction to mixed strategies. See also Rasmussen 1989 (chap. 3).

$$R_1(\cdot) = R \quad \alpha > 0.5$$

$$R_1(\cdot) = L \quad \alpha < 0.5$$

$$R_1(\cdot) = (0.5, 0.5) \quad \alpha = 0.5.$$

Likewise, Player 2's best reply correspondence is where β equals the probability that Player 1 plays L:

$$R_2(\cdot) = R \quad \beta > 0.5$$

$$R_2(\cdot) = L \quad \beta < 0.5$$

$$R_2(\cdot) = (0.5, 0.5) \quad \beta = 0.5.$$

In the prior examples, we have provided a game with one pure strategy Nash equilibrium and another game with two pure strategy Nash equilibria and a mixed strategy equilibrium. In the next example, we present a case in which the only equilibrium is a mixed strategy equilibrium. This game is presented in matrix 3. With any pure strategy combination, one of the players has an incentive to change strategies. Thus, no pure strategy equilibrium exists.

A mixed strategy equilibrium does exist in this game. This mixed strategy equilibrium is $\{(0.5, 0.5), (0.5, 0.5)\}$. If one player decided to unilaterally change his strategy, his payoff would be no better than that yielded by this combination. In addition, the other player would have an incentive to change her strategy. For example, the payoff function for Player 1 of this game is

$$P_1(\alpha, \beta) = \beta - 2\alpha\beta + 2$$

where α is the probability that Player 2 will choose L and β is the probability that Player 1 will choose L. If α is 0.5, then the best expected payoff Player 1 can receive is 2. This expected payoff results from any possible mixed strategy by Player 1. However, if Player 1 chooses a strategy different from $(0.5, 0.5)$, Player 2 has an incentive to change strategies. This can be seen by examining Player 2's payoff function, which is presented in the following equation:

$$P_2(\alpha, \beta) = 2\alpha\beta - \alpha - 2\beta + 3$$

where α is the probability that Player 2 will choose L and β is the probability that Player 1 will choose L. If β is .5, then Player 2's

Player 2

	L	*R*
L	1,2	3,1
R	2,2	2,3

Player 1 *L*

Player 1 *R*

Matrix 3. A matrix game with no pure strategy equilibrium

expected payoff is 2 regardless of what mix she chooses. On the other hand, if β is 0.75, Player 2's optimal mix would be (1,0), that is, play *L* with certainty. Likewise, if β is 0.25, Player 2's optimal mix would (0,1), that is, play *R* with certainty. These responses by Player 2 to Player 1's strategy choice can be calculated by using the preceding payoff function. If Player 1 sets β at 0.75, then Player 1's payoff function becomes

$$P_2(\alpha, 0.75) = 0.5\alpha + 1.5.$$

This expression is maximized by setting α equal to 1. If Player 1 set β at 0.25, then Player 1's payoff function becomes

$$P_2(\alpha, 0.25) = -0.5\alpha + 2.5.$$

This expression is maximized by setting α equal to 0. Thus, a change from the mix of (0.5,0.5) leads the other player to also change his or her mix. The only mixed strategy equilibrium in this game, then, is $\{(0.5,0.5),(0.5,0.5)\}$.

Thus far we have shown what a mixed strategy equilibrium is. However, we have not illustrated how to find a mixed strategy equilibrium. If you study matrix 3, you will observe that there is no pure strategy equilibrium. To find a mixed strategy equilibrium in this game, one first must calculate Player 1's expected values for playing *L* and *R* and then set these expectations equal to each other. When we solve for β (where this represents the probability of Player 1 playing *L*), the probability that is yielded provides us with the mixed strategy for Player 1 when Player 2 is indifferent between playing *L* or *R*. The relevant expectations are

$$EP_1(L) = \alpha 1 + (1 - \alpha)3$$

and

$$EP_1(R) = \alpha 2 + (1 - \alpha)2.$$

Setting these two equations equal, we find that α equals $1/2$. Thus, Player 1 will be indifferent between playing L and R when Player 2 chooses to play the mixed strategy $(0.5, 0.5)$. Since this is a symmetric game, one can show that Player 2 will be indifferent between L and R when Player 1 chooses the mixed strategy $(0.5, 0.5)$. Thus, $\{(0.5, 0.5), (0.5, 0.5)\}$ is a Nash equilibrium.

Games can have two types of equilibrium: pure strategy and mixed strategy. Each game has at least one equilibrium.[4] However, many games, as shown in this section, have more than one equilibrium.

There are other ways to represent the games presented in the preceding. For example, one could represent these games in extensive form. This form is examined later in this chapter. It is sometimes more convenient and/or useful to model a game in extensive form instead of matrix form. To motivate the usefulness of matrix versus extensive form games, a brief case study is presented in the next section. This case concerns the destruction of the ANZUS alliance. Following a description of the case, three sections show how this case can be studied with matrix games, repeated games, and extensive form games.

A Brief Examination of the Decline of ANZUS

The U.S. Department of State on February 4, 1985, announced that New Zealand had turned down an American request for the destroyer *Buchanan* to pay one of its ports a call. This action followed the New Zealand election of July 1984 in which the Labour Party and its leader, David Lange, took control of Parliament. One of the planks of this party's platform advocated that New Zealand be declared a nuclear free zone: no nuclear weapons would be allowed on its lands or in its territorial waters. Thus, when the Pentagon requested permission for a destroyer to pay a New Zealand port a call, the New Zealand government refused to allow the ship into port without an American guarantee that it did not carry nuclear weapons. The United States, for

---

4. In fact, all games have at least one Nash equilibrium (Nash 1950, 1951).

security reasons, refused to acknowledge whether the ship had nuclear weapons. Without this guarantee New Zealand would not allow the ship to enter port.

During the next three months, relations between New Zealand and the United States became more troubled. On February 4, the United States cancelled the ANZUS "Sea Eagle" exercise. A State Department official stated that: "The denial of port access would be a matter of grave concern which goes to the core of our mutual obligations to our allies" (*New York Times*, February 6, 1985). Secretary of Defense Caspar Weinberger, while testifying before the Senate Armed Services Committee on February 4, warned New Zealand that its actions "constituted a serious attack upon the effectiveness of an alliance which is absolutely essential to the security of New Zealand" (*Washington Post*, February 5, 1985). He also stated that Prime Minister Lange was setting "a course which can only be of great harm to themselves, and I hope they'll change it" (*Washington Post*, February 5, 1985).

The United States withdrew from a joint New Zealand–United States antisubmarine exercise on February 19. Secretary of State George Schultz, testifying before the Senate Budget Committee, stated that the United States was in the process of withdrawing from all military operations with New Zealand since it "has basically taken a walk" from its alliance responsibilities (*Washington Post*, February 21, 1985). It was made clear that while New Zealand was still considered a friendly government it would no longer be treated as an ally. On February 26, the United States announced that it would no longer supply New Zealand with military intelligence. On March 4, the United States and Australia announced that the ANZUS meeting scheduled for July had been canceled. Assistant Secretary for Asian and Pacific Affairs of State Paul Wolfowitz, testifying before the Subcommittee on Asian and Pacific Affairs of the House Foreign Affairs Committee, stated that: "A military alliance has little meaning without military cooperation. . . . New Zealand cannot have it both ways" (*Washington Post*, March 19, 1985). He also added that military relations with New Zealand would be restored as soon as the ban on nuclear weapons was rescinded.

How can we explain the actions of these two nations? New Zealand was faced with two options. It could have either refused to allow U.S. vessels carrying nuclear weapons into its harbors or it could have allowed such entry. Why did this country choose the former course by refusing to allow the *Buchanan* into its territorial waters? This action was not without cost. Because of the retaliation of the United States,

New Zealand on the thirteenth of June was forced to increase its military expenditures by 18 percent to compensate for the loss of protection resulting from the shelving of ANZUS. Perhaps Lange and the other leaders of New Zealand did not foresee the U.S. reaction to this situation. On February 4, Lange, reflecting this view, stated: "[ANZUS is] an association which is of long standing, its end is not currently threatened, and it is impossible even in the communication emerging from the United States to detect a threat to ANZUS" (*Washington Post*, February 5, 1985). Thus, we would not expect that the New Zealand government believed it would face immediate retaliation for excluding the *Buchanan*. This point is reinforced by a later comment of Lange's in which he said: "They are not, in my view, the kind of actions which a great power should take against a small loyal ally which has stood by it, through thick and thin, in war and peace" (*Washington Post*, February 27, 1985).

How can we explain the actions of the United States? The United States was not reacting to New Zealand's action in isolation. Other allies viewed its reaction with interest. Japan at that time had laws that prohibited nuclear weapons on its territory. However, despite the protests of the antinuclear opposition, the Japanese government had always allowed U.S. vessels to enter its harbors without inquiring whether or not they held nuclear weapons. If the United States had allowed New Zealand's actions to go unchecked, it could have had repercussions in Japan. Also, many Western European governments were facing increased pressure to remove and/or refuse the installation of American nuclear weapons within their borders. An acceptance of New Zealand's actions might have increased the chances of these arms being either removed or not installed in these European countries.

Given this situation, the United States had two strategies vis-à-vis New Zealand. It could acquiesce or it could retaliate by declaring the ANZUS treaty not binding as long as New Zealand held its present course. If it subscribed to the first option, it would be setting a precedent that could be followed by "allies that really count, the ones in NATO and, of course, Japan" (*Washington Post*, February 26, 1985). Thus, it chose to take the second course. It is clear from comments by Bernard Kalb and Prime Minister Lange that the United States had its reputation in mind when it took this action. Kalb said: "We hoped that our response to New Zealand would signal that the course of these [antinuclear and peace] movements would not be cost-free in terms of security with the United States" (*New York Times*, February 6, 1985). Lange stated on March 1 that: "We have been told by some officials in the United States administration that our decision is not, as they put it, cost-free—that we are to be made an example of and that we are to be convicted of some sort of heresy, not by our enemies, but by our allies" (*Washington Post*, March 2, 1985). Thus, the United States may have chosen to retaliate against New Zealand in order to avoid presenting the wrong image to its other allies.

In summary, New Zealand faced the following choices. It could either refuse U.S. ships carrying nuclear weapons entry into its territorial waters or it could allow such entry. If New Zealand chose to exclude U.S. vessels, the United States faced two choices. It could either acquiesce to the new demand by New Zealand or it could retaliate.

In this section, we have presented a brief discussion of the interaction between the United States and New Zealand immediately after the elections of Prime Minister Lange. This case study will be used throughout the rest of this chapter to illustrate different game theory techniques. We begin this discussion by considering matrix form games.

Matrix Form Games

In this section, our discussion of matrix form games is expanded from that of our earlier presentation. In addition, we use the ANZUS example developed in the previous section to motivate our discussion of this type of game.

The application of game theory to political science has been dominated by the use of a pair of 2×2 games, that is, the Prisoners' Dilemma and Chicken. Other 2×2 games have been considered to lesser degrees, that is, Stag Hunt and Assurance. Most political scientists possess at least passing familiarity with the first two games. As such, we will not consider them at this point in the book. The other two games are thoroughly discussed in chapter 4. Instead of considering these four games, the task for this section is to develop games that are connected with the interaction between the United States and New Zealand as described in the ANZUS example.

Matrix 4 is a matrix form representation of the interactions between the United States and New Zealand. The game shown in this figure applies to the case in which decision makers in the United States are myopic.[5] First, note that each player has two strategies. New Zealand can either acquiesce (*A*) or rebel (*R*); the United States

---

5. By myopic, we mean that they do not take into account how their actions at this point in time might affect their future interactions with New Zealand as well as other states. Repetitions and the addition of actors will be addressed in subsequent sections of this chapter.

New Zealand

	A	R
A United States **P**	$b,b - c$ $b - p,-c - d$	$0,b$ $-p,-d$

For New Zealand: $b > b - c > -d > -c - d$
For the United States: $b > b - p > 0 > -p$

Matrix 4. A matrix game involving the United States and New Zealand

can either acquiesce (A) or punish (P). The payoff each actor connects with the interaction of two strategies is presented in the box of the matrix representing this interaction.

We will begin the analysis of this game by developing the payoffs of each player. New Zealand's best outcome occurs when it receives the benefit of the alliance without any of the costs, that is, remaining in the alliance and not allowing U.S. vessels with nuclear weapons into its ports. This payoff is represented by b. Its next worst outcome occurs when it acquiesces to the demands of the United States. In this case, it still receives the benefits of the alliance while allowing the United States to freely send vessels into its ports. This payoff is represented by $b - c$. The next worst payoff arises when it decides to refuse U.S. vessels free entry into its ports and the United States retaliates for such actions. This payoff is represented by $-d$. The least preferred alternative arises from the inability of matrix form games to exclude nonsensical strategy combinations. This occurs when New Zealand allows U.S. vessels entry into its ports but the United States still punishes its ally. The payoff in this situation is $-c - d$.

What about the United States? The United States' most preferred outcome arises when both nations acquiesce. In this case, it receives the payoff of b. Its next most preferred outcome occurs when New Zealand allows U.S. vessels into its ports and the United States still punishes. In this case, it receives $b - p$. The next most preferred outcome arises when New Zealand rebels and the United States acquiesces to this rebellion. In this case, the payoff is 0. The worst outcome for the United States occurs when it chooses to punish New Zealand for its choice to exclude U.S. naval vessels. In this case, the United States loses the benefits of the alliance as well as incurring the cost of punishing New Zealand. This payoff is represented by $-p$.

In this game, both the United States and New Zealand have *dominant strategies.* A strategy is dominant if it is a player's strictly best response to any strategies the other players might choose. In other words, the dominant strategy is one that yields the player her highest payoff given the strategy choice of the other players. There are actually two types of domination in game theory. We can talk of strictly dominating strategies and weakly dominating strategies. Our previous informal definition of a dominant strategy is actually the definition of a strictly dominant strategy. On the other hand, a strategy is a *weakly dominant strategy* if it does at least as well as any other strategy against all possible strategies chosen by other players and if it sometimes does better.

If each actor plays her dominant strategy, the resulting outcome is New Zealand restricting access to its ports and the United States not retaliating against this action. This outcome arises from the Nash equilibrium of the game. A *Nash equilibrium* is an equilibrium if no actor has an incentive to change her strategy unilaterally once each player has chosen her component of the Nash equilibrium as her strategy choice. In the game in Matrix 4, neither actor has an incentive to unilaterally change his or her strategy from $\{A,R\}$. Neither would do better by unilaterally changing to A in the case of New Zealand or P in the case of the United States.

There are other factors that may be integrated into our game theoretic framework. This game can be changed in three ways. First, if the United States chose to punish New Zealand for its rebellion, this would lead us to believe that the United States was reacting to the actions of New Zealand. We would not expect the United States to punish New Zealand if that nation did not rebel. The actors, then, were not acting simultaneously; rather, they were acting sequentially. The common manner for considering such situations is with extensive form games, which will be considered elsewhere in this chapter. However, one can consider these situations with a matrix form game.

A second factor may be that the payoffs of the game are incorrectly specified. If the United States explicitly took into account the effects of its decision on the calculations of other allies, the payoffs of this game would be different.[6] For example, the United States may believe that punishing New Zealand's rebellion would deter other nations from acting similarly. As such, the cost of punishing this rebellion may not be as costly as was represented in the preceding analysis.

Or, third, we could explicitly take into account the actions of other players or repeated play between the two players in the game. To do this, we would have to create an N-person game that would include New Zealand, the United States, and its other allies, or create a repeated game involving New Zealand and the United States.[7] This change will be considered in the next section. In considering the other two changes to this game, we will consider changes in payoffs first and then will examine sequential moves with a matrix form game.

Modeling Sequential Moves within a Matrix Game

An alternative form of the game is shown in matrix 5. This form considers a situation in which the decision makers in the United States consider the effects of their decision on the calculations of other allies. For example, decision makers would take into account the effect of their decision on the choices of their European allies to base cruise missiles in their nations. The only difference between this game and the one represented in matrix 4 occurs in the lower right hand box. Here, the payoff for the United States changes from $-p$ to $-p + r$. The r term reflects the rewards the United States gains in its reputation from punishing this rebellion.

In this case, New Zealand still possesses a dominant strategy. However, the United States no longer has a dominant strategy. In this game, the Nash equilibrium occurs when New Zealand rebels and the United States punishes this rebellion.

There are some problems with even this game and its resulting solution. The most obvious is that this approach neglects the fact that New Zealand and the United States did not act simultaneously. New Zealand moved first, and the United States reacted. However, the representations in matrices 4 and 5 do not take this sequence into account. To take the orders of moves into account, one would have to

---

6. Another way to take into account the effects of U.S. actions on other players is to develop this game as a repeated game. The repetition could involve either repeated interactions between the United States and New Zealand or interactions between the United States and other nations. This notion will be considered in a later section.

7. We have combined repeated and N-person games here because they can be considered as similar in some circumstances. For example, see Kreps and Wilson 1982 and Milgrom and Roberts 1982.

New Zealand

	A	R
A United States	$b,b-c$	$0,b$
P	$b-p,-c-d$	$-p+r,-d$

For New Zealand: $b > b - c > -d > -c - d$
For the United States: $b > b - p > -p + r > 0$

Matrix 5. A revised matrix game involving the United States and New Zealand

allow the United States to have conditional strategies. For example, the United States could have a strategy that allows it to punish New Zealand if it rebels and acquiesce if New Zealand does the same. Matrix 6 represents the conditional strategy of the game presented in matrix 4.

The United States no longer chooses just one action. Instead, it chooses an action depending on what New Zealand does. For example, the second strategy available to the United States is (A,P). This means that if New Zealand chose A the United States would choose A and if New Zealand chose R the United States would choose P. Thus, the first component of U.S. strategy represents what it does if New Zealand chooses A, while the second component represents what it does if New Zealand chooses R.

In this game, New Zealand no longer has a dominant strategy. However, the United States does have a weakly dominant strategy. This is (A,A). A Nash equilibrium in this game is $\{(A,A),R\}$. Neither party has an incentive to unilaterally change strategies with this strategy combination. There are two other pure strategy Nash equilibria in this game. These are $\{(A,P),A\}$ and $\{(P,A),R\}$. None of these equilibria corresponds to the actual events that transpired between the United States and New Zealand.

We could also represent the game in matrix 5 in which sequence is taken into account. This game then becomes the one represented in matrix 7. The United States has a weakly dominant strategy in this game. This strategy is (A,P). One of the Nash equilibria of this game

New Zealand

	A	R
A,A	$b,b-c$	$0,b$
A,P	$b,b-c$	$-p,-d$
P,A	$b-p,-c-d$	$0,b$
P,P	$b-p,-c-d$	$-p,-d$

United States (row label for the matrix)

For New Zealand: $b > b - c > -d > -c - d$
For the United States: $b > b - p > 0 > -p$

Matrix 6. A matrix game with sequential moves involving the United States and New Zealand

is then $\{(A,P),A\}$. Of course, this is not what occurred in our case. The other Nash equilibrium is $\{(P,P),R\}$. The strategy of the United States seems unreasonable. Why would the United States choose to punish New Zealand if New Zealand did *not* exclude U.S. naval vessels from its ports? Thus, even the use of conditional strategies does not eliminate one of the problems noted with our original game.

It is unusual to model a sequential process with a matrix form game. Instead, we will examine it from an extensive form game perspective. Before beginning our consideration of extensive form games, it is important to reexamine the games in matrices 6 and 7. If the United States had a weakly dominant strategy, why did a Nash equilibrium exist in each game that did not use this weakly dominant strategy? To answer this question, consider the nature of a weakly dominant strategy. Unlike a strictly dominant strategy, a player will not always receive a better payoff from playing a weakly dominant

New Zealand

	A	R
A,A	$b,b-c$	$0,b$
A,P	$b,b-c$	$-p+r,-d$
P,A	$b-p,-c-d$	$0,b$
P,P	$b-p,-c-d$	$-p+r,-d$

United States

For New Zealand: $b > b - c > -d > -c - d$
For the United States: $b > b - p > -p + r > 0$

Matrix 7. A revised matrix game with sequential moves involving the United States and New Zealand

strategy instead of other strategies. This fact is what allows us to have more than one Nash equilibrium in these games, and two of the Nash equilibria result when the United States does not choose to play its weakly dominant strategy.

In the next section, we consider the sequential nature of this game more thoroughly. This discussion is accomplished through the development of extensive form games.

Extensive Form Games

Extensive form games provide another approach for applying game theory to political situations. This approach is very flexible in that it can be used to model sequential and simultaneous decision choices. In addition, we are able to consider situations in which the actors possess different levels of information about the game. Through the continued use of the ANZUS case, these applications of the extensive form are considered in the following.

The extensive form is a very natural way to model. The sequence of play is explicitly portrayed and can easily be seen in this form of the game. The extensive form game is also quite versatile. All situations that can be considered with a matrix form game can also be considered with an extensive form game. In addition, different levels of information can be considered in this game. While these considerations can also be addressed in a matrix form game, the representation of these characteristics in this form can be awkward.

A simple extensive form game is presented in figure 1. This game may remind the reader of decision trees. However, there is a key difference between decision trees and game trees. A decision tree represents the choice opportunities of a single player. A game tree, on the other hand, represents the choice opportunities of two or more players. The relationship between a myopic United States and New Zealand is portrayed in this figure. This is an extensive form game representation of the game modeled in matrix 4 with one key difference. The game in figure 1 clearly identifies the sequence of decisions that transpired between these two countries. The first decision is made by New Zealand. The United States then moves with knowledge of the relevant actors and the action taken by New Zealand. In matrix 4, the two actors were, for all practical purposes, moving simultaneously. The United States chose its strategy without the knowledge of what action New Zealand had taken.

The game in figure 1 is one of perfect information while the game in matrix 4 is one of imperfect information. The difference is the information that is available to the United States. A game of perfect information is one in which a player moving in the game knows what moves all previous players have made. Of course, such games can also be examined using matrix form games. The reader should note that figure 1 is merely the extensive form representation of the game in matrix 6. A game of imperfect information is one in which a player moving in the game does not know the actions of one or more previous players. Matrix 4 presents a game of imperfect information since neither player knows the stategy chosen by the other until these strategies are revealed simultaneously.

Extensive form games are not limited to games of perfect information. One could easily model a game of imperfect information using this form. Figure 2 presents such a game. This game differs from the game presented in figure 1 because of the inclusion of an information set. This information set, denoted in figure 2 by a broken

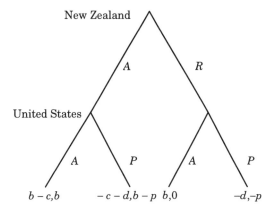

New Zealand $b > b - c > -d > -c - d$

United States $b > b - p > -p + r > 0 > -p$

Fig. 1. An extensive form game involving the United States and New Zealand with perfect information

line, is used to show that the United States does not know what decision New Zealand had made. An information set denotes what information a player has about the actions of players who move before him. A node or decision node is the point at which one of the players makes a decision. An information set may contain one or more nodes. If a game consists of an information set composed of singletons, that is, containing only one node, we refer to this game as a game of perfect information. If any information set within a game is not a singleton, then the game is one of imperfect information. The game in figure 2 is definitely one of imperfect information since the United States possesses a nonsingleton information set. The United States does not know whether New Zealand has chosen to acquiesce or rebel.

Returning to figure 1, we should examine the equilibria in this game. The payoffs of this game are identical to those in matrix 4. As such, we will not repeat their discussion here. The equilibrium for this game can be found by using backwards induction. Backwards induction refers to a technique in which one analyzes the game by moving from the node or information set of the last decision maker to that of the next actor. This continues until either you have reached the information set of the first actor to move or an information set does not allow you to move further. For example, New Zealand when making

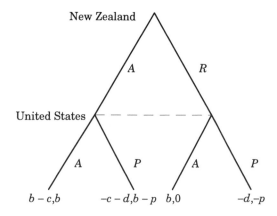

New Zealand $b > b - c > -d > -c - d$

United States $b > b - p > -p + r > 0 > -p$

Fig. 2. An extensive form game involving the United States and New Zealand with imperfect information

its choice will take into account what the United States will do with its subsequent move. Thus, New Zealand will examine the payoffs for the United States in each of its two subgames. If the United States had to choose between acquiescing and punishing after New Zealand chose to acquiesce, it would choose to acquiesce. This would result in a payoff of $b - c$ for New Zealand. If New Zealand, on the other hand, chose to rebel, the United States would still choose to respond by acquiescing. This choice would yield a payoff of b for New Zealand. Since b is greater than $b - p$, New Zealand would choose to rebel given the expected reaction of the United States. Thus, this game is solved by examining what each player will do given the potential actions of subsequent players.

What is the Nash equilibrium of this game? Thus far we have described the payoffs of a Nash equilibrium. However, we have not presented the strategies that would lead one to this payoff. An easy answer to this question would be $\{R,A\}$. However, this combination does not fully represent the strategy space available to the United States. The U.S. strategy should represent what it would do depending on the choice of New Zealand. In other words, the U.S. strategy should consist of two choices. The first would represent the U.S. response to New Zealand choosing to rebel, while the second would represent its response to New Zealand choosing to acquiesce. Thus, any of the following two strategy combinations can yield this outcome. These are {R,(A,A)} and {R,(P,A)}.

This game, of course, is the same one as presented in table 6. There we presented a matrix representation of this game. In that game, we identified the two equilibria as well as a third equilibrium, that is, {A,(A,P)}. This third strategy combination calls for the United States to commit to punishing New Zealand for rebelling. Of course, if New Zealand actually chose to rebel, the United States would be better off acquiescing. But if New Zealand chooses to acquiesce, the United States would have no reason to unilaterally change its strategy, and New Zealand could not be made better off by unilaterally changing its own strategy. While this strategy combination is then a Nash equilibrium, it does not seem reasonable.

Can we distinguish between this equilibrium and the other two? We can make this distinction by using a common refinement of the Nash equilibrium concept. These refinements have been developed in order to distinguish between the multitude of Nash equilibria that can result in a game. The most common refinement is that of a subgame perfect equilibrium. A subgame perfect equilibrium allows us to distinguish between these three equilibria. Before defining subgame perfect equilibrium, we need to define a subgame. A subgame (actually a proper subgame) is any subset of the complete game tree, that (1) begins with an information set that is a singleton for all players, (2) includes all subsequent nodes, and (3) ends with the associated payoffs.[8] Note that this means that an entire game is always a subgame and that a subgame cannot cross any player's information set. From this definition of a subgame, a subgame perfect equilibrium can be defined as a strategy that is an equilibrium for all subgames of a game. In other words, a subgame perfect equilibrium of a game is a Nash equilibrium that holds for all subgames.[9]

Is {A,(A,P)} a subgame perfect equilibrium? This is not a subgame perfect equilibrium. This can be seen by examining the subgame that results when New Zealand decides to rebel. In the resulting subgame, the United States has a dominant strategy to acquiesce to this rebellion. The choice of punishment would make the United States worse off at this point. Thus, while his combination is a Nash

---

8. For more discussion, see Friedman 1986 (77–82), Tirole 1988 (428–29), or Rasmussen 1989 (83–85)

9. For more details of subgame perfect equilibrium, see Selten 1975, Friedman 1986 (77–82), or Tirole 1988 (428–31).

equilibrium, it is not subgame perfect. This refined has allowed us to eliminate a Nash equilibrium which arises because of a noncredible commitment.

What about the two remaining Nash equilibria? These are $\{R,(A,A)\}$ and $\{R,(P,A)\}$. Are both of these Nash equilibria also subgame perfect equilibria? We will examine each equilibrium individually. $\{R,(A,A)\}$ is a subgame perfect equilibrium. In order for it to be an equilibrium, A must be the equilibrium strategy for each subgame of the game for the United States. In both subgames, the United States receives a better payoff from playing acquiesce than from punishing. This strategy combination then defines a subgame perfect equilibrium since neither party would want to unilaterally change strategies and since it represents an equilibrium for each subgame of the game.

On the other hand, $\{R,(P,A)\}$ is not a subgame perfect equilibrium. If the subgame was reached that resulted from New Zealand playing acquiesce, the United States is made worse off by playing punish than by playing acquiesce. Thus, this strategy combination does not define an equilibrium for each subgame of this game. The United States would have an incentive to change strategies unilaterally if the subgame is reached in which New Zealand plays acquiesce. The Nash equilibrium that is excluded in this manner is one that lies off the equilibrium path. In other words, it is excluded because of the proposed action of the United States when New Zealand chooses not to play its equilibrium strategy.

Recapping the following analysis, we have introduced the reader to extensive form games, games of perfect information, subgames, and subgame perfect equilibrium. With these concepts in mind, we will analyze another extensive form game. This game is also a game of perfect information. It differs from the game in figure 1 in that the payoffs have been changed to reflect those that were developed in matrix 5. This game is presented in figure 3.

If New Zealand chose to acquiesce, the United States would choose to respond with aquiesce, which would result in a payoff of $b - c$ for New Zealand. If New Zealand chose to rebel, the United States would respond by punishing, which would yield New Zealand a payoff of $-d$. New Zealand would then choose to acquiesce. Given this choice, the United States would respond with acquiesce. The Nash equilibrium that would represent this behavior is $\{A,(A,P)\}$. This strategy combination is also a subgame perfect equilibrium since the U.S. strategy choice is a Nash equilibrium for each subgame of the game.

There is another Nash equilibrium in this game. This strategy

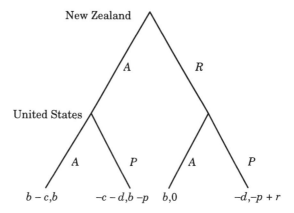

New Zealand $b > b - c > -d > -c - d$

United States $b > b - p > -p + r > 0 > -p$

Fig. 3. A revised extensive form game involving the United States and New Zealand with perfect information

pair, $\{R,(P,P)\}$, is not a subgame perfect equilibrium. This is because the United States would prefer to play acquiesce instead of punish if New Zealand chose to acquiesce. Thus, there is only one subgame perfect equilibrium in this game.

Thus far, we have considered cases in which New Zealand knew with certainty what the payoffs of the United States were. However, it could be the case that there is uncertainty in New Zealand concerning the payoffs of the United States. These payoffs could be those presented in figure 3 or those presented in figure 1. Such a game would be one of incomplete information. A game of complete information is one in which each player knows the following: (1) who the other players are, (2) all strategies available to these players, and (3) the other players' payoffs with certainty. A game of incomplete information results when one or more of these conditions do not hold. The most common form of a game of incomplete information is one in which a player does not know other players' payoffs with certainty. We now turn to analyzing the interaction between New Zealand and the United States from this perspective.

Extensive form games are well suited for modeling games of incomplete information. The typical manner in which incomplete information is treated in extensive form games is through the introduction of Nature. Nature is portrayed as moving first and is unobserved by at least one of the players. Nature serves to determine a player's type, which includes strategy set, information partitions, and payoff functions.[10] One player, then, does not know the type of the other player. From our ANZUS example, New Zealand would not know whether it was facing a United States that prefers to acquiesce when New Zealand rebels or a United States that prefers to punish when a rebellion occurs. In game theoretic terms, the United States then can be one of two types.

Using this conceptualization of Nature in a game of incomplete information, the extensive form can be used to integrate both of the basic games previously developed concerning the interaction between New Zealand and the United States. Figure 4 depicts the relationship between the United States and New Zealand in an extensive form game with one-sided information.[11] In this game, the United States possesses either payoffs from figure 1 or the payoffs from figure 3. The game is one of one-sided incomplete information since the United States knows its own payoff structure as well as that of New Zealand but New Zealand does not know the payoffs of the United States. Instead, New Zealand believes with a probability of α that the United States possesses the payoffs from figure 1. This is represented in figure 4 with an information set that envelopes New Zealand's decision nodes. This indicates that New Zealand possesses incomplete information concerning the payoffs of the United States.

What are the equilibria of this game? And do the equilibria depend on the value of α? In finding the equilibria, we can once again use backwards induction to partially solve this game. In all but one of the subgames, the United States would choose A over P. Thus, New Zealand faces the tree in figure 5 when it is deciding between its two strategies.

Unlike the previous games, the equilibrium of this game depends on New Zealand's subjective estimate of α. This is caused by the fact that New Zealand does not have a dominant strategy in this game. If Nature chooses the first option, then New Zealand's best choice would be R. On the other hand, if Nature chooses the second option, then New Zealand's best choice would be A. Thus, the choice of New Zealand is conditional on its perceptions of the type of United States it is facing. Is it facing the type with payoffs from figure 1 or is it facing the type with payoffs from figure 3? For convenience, we will label

---

10. See Rasmussen 1989 (48–54).

11. Games of one-sided incomplete information are also referred to as games of asymmetric information. Banks (1991) provides an excellent review of the uses of this modeling technique in political science.

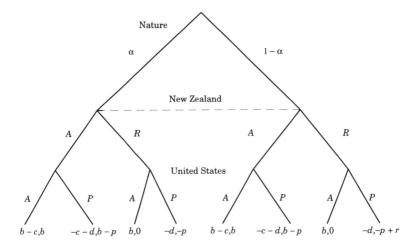

New Zealand $b > b - c > -d > -c - d$

United States $b > b - p > -p + r > 0 > -p$

Fig. 4. An extensive form game involving the United States and New Zealand with incomplete information

the former Type I and the latter type Type II. From our substantive discussion of this case earlier in the chapter, a Type I United States was the type of actor that New Zealand was expecting to face. New Zealand did not expect the United States to retaliate against its decision to keep ships with nuclear weapons out of its ports. However, New Zealand seemed to face a United States that acted as if it were a Type II. This United States chose to punish New Zealand's rebellion.

New Zealand, in this way, is facing an expected payoff problem. In other words, it does not know which game it is playing with certainty unless α equals 0 or 1. It must make a choice between two potential outcomes that can occur with a given probability. Thus, New Zealand needs to compare the expected value of R with that of A in order to choose between the two strategies. New Zealand needs to discover the values of α for which the expected payoff of acquiesce is greater than that of rebel and those values for which the expected value of rebel is greater than that of acquiesce. In order to do so, we have created the following inequality in which the expression to the left of the inequality is the expected value of R and the value to the right of the inequality is the expected value of acquiesce:

$$\alpha b + (1 - \alpha)(-d) > \alpha(b - c) + (1 - \alpha)(b - c).$$

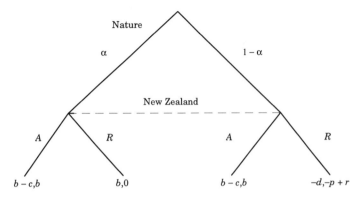

New Zealand $b > b - c > -d > -c - d$

United States $b > b - p > -p + r > 0 > -p$

Fig. 5. The reduced form of the game in figure 4

This reduces to:

$$\alpha > \frac{(b + d - c)}{(b + d)}.$$

New Zealand should choose R if this inequality holds; if not, it should choose A. Before proceeding to characterize the equilibrium of this game, we need to consider whether the restraint on α is a real one. In other words, can the fraction on the right side of the second inequality take on values between 0 and 1? From New Zealand's payoffs, we know that $b - c$ is greater than $-d$. As such, we know that $b + d$ is greater than c. Thus, the numerator of this fraction must always be positive and less than the denominator. This inequality then puts a meaningful restraint on α.

The equilibria of this game depend on New Zealand's beliefs concerning the value of α as well as the actual type of payoffs the United States possesses. Thus, the equilibria can be characterized as follows.

1. If the United States is of Type I, then

$$\{A,(A,A)\} \quad \text{if } \alpha < \frac{(b + d - c)}{(b + d)}$$

$$\{R,(A,A)\} \quad \text{if } \alpha > \frac{(b + d - c)}{(b + d)}.$$

2. If the United States is of Type II, then

$$\{A,(A,P)\} \quad \text{if } \alpha < \frac{(b + d - c)}{(b + d)}$$

$$\{R,(A,P)\} \quad \text{if } \alpha > \frac{(b + d - c)}{(b + d)}.$$

To illustrate why these combinations are equilibria, examine the first equilibrium.[12] If the United States is a Type I player, it has no incentive to deviate from the strategy combination of (A,A) since it receives its best payoffs from this choice. New Zealand also has no incentive to deviate since its expected value of playing A is higher than its expected value of playing R in this case. Since neither party has an incentive to change strategies unilaterally this is an equilibrium.

Unlike our previous games, if the United States is a Type II player, this one does result in an equilibrium in which New Zealand rebels and the United States punishes the rebellion. Thus, we have finally discovered an equilibrium that is similar to the actual outcome of the interaction between the United States and New Zealand. Examining this equilibrium further, one might suppose that New Zealand would want to change its strategy to A given the response of the United States. After the fact, New Zealand may well have regretted its actions. However, this regret occurs because New Zealand now possesses knowledge of what type the United States is. Without this knowledge, it can only use α as an estimate of this type.

What would happen if New Zealand could not directly observe the United States' type, but it could observe actions taken by the United States? Could New Zealand use these actions to gain a better estimate of what type it is facing? The game in figure 4 is transformed with some minor changes to the one presented in figure 6. In this game, Nature again moves first to select the type of the United States. The United States, knowing its type, then announces its policy. It can announce that it will punish (P) or it can choose to acquiesce (A). New Zealand then acts. It can decide to acquiesce (A) or rebel (R). New Zealand has complete knowledge of the announced actions of the United States; it does not possess any knowledge of Nature's choice except for the probabilities that Nature chooses the United States to be

12. There is a mixed strategy equilibrium in which $\alpha = [(b + d - c)/(b + d)]$. We do not explore the topic of mixed equilibria in this type of game in this chapter. This topic is considered in chapter 5.

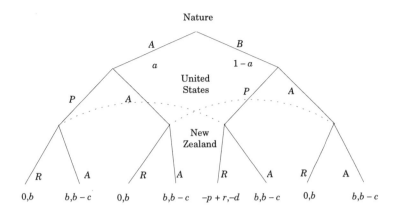

New Zealand $b > b - c > -d > -c - d$

United States $b > b - p > -p + r > 0 > -p$

Fig. 6. A game of incomplete information between the United States and New Zealand

a Type I or Type II nation. These probabilities are, respectively, α and $1 - \alpha$. After New Zealand chooses its action, the United States can then decide to change its policy. For instance, a Type II United States could choose P initially and then change this policy to A if New Zealand chooses A.[13]

By adding a second choice for the United States, there is the possibility that the United States may try to bluff. This ability to bluff arises from the fact that the United States can choose without cost a different action after New Zealand has acted. For example, a Type I United States could choose P initially and then change this policy to A regardless of New Zealand's choice. New Zealand, not knowing the type it is confronting, must somehow decide whether the United States is bluffing, that is, whether it is Type I or Type II. How should New Zealand react to this potential for bluffing? According to game theorists, a commonly accepted way would be to use the United States' announced strategy as well as its action to update its probability of α, that is, the probability that the United States is a Type I

---

13. This second choice is not shown in figure 6 because we assume that the United States will makes its optimal choice at each end node.

nation. Game theorists have traditionally used Bayes' theorem for the updating of beliefs.[14] The form of Bayes' Theorem used in this process is as follows:

P(Type I | Punish)

$$= \frac{P(\text{Punish} \mid \text{Type I})P(\text{Type I})}{P(\text{Punish} \mid \text{Type II})P(\text{Type II}) + P(\text{Punish} \mid \text{Type I})P(\text{Type I})}. \quad (2.1)$$

The conditional probability that is calculated from this expression provides New Zealand with an updated estimate of the probability that the United States is a Type I nation given that it chose punish as its first action. These calculations are dependent on the choice of strategies of the United States since this choice leads New Zealand to assign values to the conditional probabilities on the right-hand side of the equation. Thus, this updated estimate is dependent on the announced strategies of the United States as well as New Zealand's initial beliefs concerning α, that is, P(Type I). After calculating this Bayesian estimate, New Zealand would use it to calculate the expected value of playing its strategy versus the expected value of all alternative strategies. It would, of course, choose the strategy that provided it with the highest expected payoff.

We now proceed to work through a case using figure 6 to illustrate how Bayesian updating can be used in deciding whether a set of strategies is an equilibrium. We will examine the following strategy combination:[15]

(1) The United States chooses P if Nature chooses A.
  chooses P if Nature chooses B.
(2) New Zealand chooses R if the United States has chosen A.
  chooses A if the United States has chosen P.

To determine whether this is an equilibrium, we will use the form of Bayes' Theorem presented above to calculate the probability that the United States is a Type I if it announces it will P. The values for the right-hand side of equation 2.1 can be developed easily from the game

14. However, not all game theorists are satisfied with standard applications of Bayes' theorem. For example, see Binmore 1993.

15. For ease of discussion, we have chosen not to present the United States' response to New Zealand as a separate strategy. Instead, the reader should assume that the strategies presented concerning this game include the optimal response by the United States to New Zealand's action. For example, assume that in this case the United States would choose at the final stage to acquiesce to New Zealand if it chose acquiesce.

and the above strategies. P(Type I) and P(Type II) are, respectively, α and $1 - \alpha$. The conditional probability $P(P \mid$ Type II$)$ equals 1 since the strategy of the United States calls for it to choose P with certainty if Nature chooses A, that is, the United States is a Type I nation. Similarly, the conditional probability $P(P \mid$ Type I$)$ equals 1. Thus, equation 2.1 becomes

$$P(\text{Type I} \mid \text{Punish}) = \frac{1(\alpha)}{[1(1 - \alpha)] + 1(\alpha)}. \tag{2.2}$$

The conditional probability P(Type I $\mid P$) then equals α. It can then be easily shown that P(Type II $\mid P$) then equals $1 - \alpha$. Before proceeding to calculate the expected values for New Zealand, the reader should note that the updated probability in this particular case is no different than the initial ones. In other words, no additional information was gleaned from the action of the United States.[16]

Given these probabilities, should New Zealand choose to change its strategies? Clearly, New Zealand has no reason to change its first option. Since the United States will not choose A, New Zealand does not gain any advantage by choosing A instead of R. It does need to examine its choices concerning a response to the United States' announcement of P. Thus, we need to examine the $E(R \mid P)$ and $E(A \mid P)$. These expected values are

$$
\begin{aligned}
E(R \mid P) &= b(\alpha) + (-d)(1 - \alpha) \\
&= \alpha b + \alpha d - d \\
&= \alpha(b + d) - d \\
E(A \mid P) &= (b - c)(\alpha) + (b - c)(1 - \alpha) \\
&= \alpha b - \alpha c + b - c - \alpha b + \alpha c \\
&= b - c.
\end{aligned}
$$

Comparing these expected values, we find that

$$
\begin{aligned}
E(R \mid P) &> E(A \mid P) \\
\alpha(b + d) - d &> b - c.
\end{aligned}
$$

Solving for α yields

$$\alpha > \frac{b + d - c}{b + d} \tag{2.3}$$

16. This is not always the case. Other cases in this chapter and in chapters 5 and 6 present situations in which the initial probabilities differ from their updated counterparts.

Thus, New Zealand will choose R if α exceeds this value on the right-hand side of equation 2.3. Given this choice by New Zealand, the United States will change its strategy. Instead of choosing P if Nature chose A, it would choose to A. This is because its payoff for the P in this situation would be b instead of 0.

On the other hand, if α is less than the value in equation 2.3, New Zealand would not change its strategy since the expected value of acquiescing is greater than that of rebelling. This set of strategies would then be an equilibrium. However, the equilibrium is not fully specified by the set of strategies since it is also dependent on the beliefs of the players concerning α. Thus, properly stated the equilibrium of this game would be

(1) The United States chooses to P if Nature chooses A.
   chooses to P if Nature chooses B.
(2) New Zealand chooses to R if the United States has chosen A.
   chooses A if the United States has chosen P.
(3) And,

$$\alpha < \frac{b + d - c}{b + d}.$$

This is a perfect Bayesian equilibrium.[17] A perfect Bayesian equilibrium consists of a set of strategies and beliefs such that the strategies for the remainder of the game follow the criteria for Nash equilibria given the beliefs and strategies of the other players, and these beliefs are based if possible on priors updated by Bayes' rules given the observed actions of the other players.

This specific perfect Bayesian equilibrium is also sometimes called a pooling equilibrium. It is a pooling equilibrium because both Type I and Type II nations will take the same actions. Thus, New Zealand will be unable to distinguish which type the United States is. If the equilibrium were differentiated between different types, then it would be called a separating equilibrium. For example, a separating equilibrium would be one in which a Type I nation would choose to acquiesce and a Type II nation would choose to punish. New Zealand would then be able to distinguish between the different types.

This is, of course, only one of the equilibria of this game. Let us examine another case, which arises from our original one. What if the

---

17. There is a mixed strategy equilibrium in which $\alpha = [(b + d - c)/(b + d)]$. We do not explore the topic of mixed equilibria in this type of game in this chapter. This topic is considered in chapter 5.

inequality in equation 2.3 holds? As stated, if Nature chooses A, the United States would choose to change its strategy to A away from P since New Zealand would choose R regardless of the actions of the United States. The new set of strategy combinations would be

(1) The United States chooses A if Nature chooses A.
                       chooses P if Nature chooses B.
(2) New Zealand chooses R if the United States has chosen A.
                       chooses R if the United States has chosen P.

If this strategy combination were an equilibrium, it would be a separating equilibrium since the United States would choose to act differently depending on its type. However, this strategy combination is not an equilibrium. Given that the United States is revealing its type in this strategy by its actions, New Zealand has no incentive to choose to rebel if the United States has chosen to punish. This can be seen by applying Bayes' Theorem in the following manner:

P(Type II | Punish)

$$= \frac{P(\text{Punish} \mid \text{Type II})P(\text{Type II})}{P(\text{Punish} \mid \text{Type II})P(\text{Type II}) + P(\text{Punish} \mid \text{Type I})P(\text{Type I})}. \qquad (2.4)$$

Substituting the values for $P(P \mid \text{Type II})$, $P(\text{Type II})$, $P(P \mid \text{Type I})$, and $P(\text{Type I})$ yields

$$P(\text{Type II} \mid \text{Punish}) = \frac{1(1 - \alpha)}{0(\alpha) + [1(1 - \alpha)]}.$$

The $P(\text{Type II} \mid P)$ then equals 1. In this case, the action of the United States did provide additional information to New Zealand. As long as the original α was not equal to 0, the action of the United States allows New Zealand to clearly recognize the type of nation it is facing.

We then calculate the following expected values:

$$E(R \mid P) = b(0) + (-d)1$$
$$= -d$$

$$E(A \mid P) = (b - c)(0) + (b - c)(1)$$
$$= b - c.$$

New Zealand then will choose its strategy, which is conditional on the United States' choice of P because the $E(A \mid P)$ is greater than the $E(R \mid P)$ since by definition $b - c$ is greater than $-d$. Thus, this strategy combination is not an equilibrium.

To find the other pure strategy equilibria in this game, one would have to test all possible sets of strategy combinations and beliefs. This would mean checking 16 strategy combinations and examining whether there are beliefs that would lead them to equilibria. While it will not be shown here, the only pure strategy equilibrium in this game is the one previously noted. Thus, this game only has a pooling equilibrium in pure strategies. Thus, substantively, the only equilibrium in pure strategies is one in which the United States is able to bluff and New Zealand is unable to detect the bluff.

Another way that New Zealand could gain information about the United States' type would be to examine the actions of the United States compared with those of other actors. For example, what if the basing of additional nuclear weapons in Europe took place before New Zealand made its decision to rebel? Or what if Japan had previously chosen to exclude naval vessels from the United States that carried nuclear weapons? If these events occurred prior to New Zealand's decision, New Zealand could have used information from these actions to update its information concerning which type of payoffs the United States possessed. Of course, the United States, knowing that future interactions could take place and knowing that its current interactions were being monitored, might act strategically to make New Zealand believe it was a Type II nation instead of Type I. If New Zealand knew that the United States was a Type II, it would not choose to rebel. This notion of repetition is explored in the next section.

Repeated Games

The notion of repetition can be addressed in a number of different ways in game theory. One could think of the United States playing the same game with New Zealand repeatedly. Or the United States could play a number of different actors sequentially in similar games. Up to this point, we have considered the interaction between the United States and New Zealand to be an isolated event, which occurs once and is never repeated. However, this is a very unrealistic way to view this and most other interactions. Very seldom does one player interact with another once and only once. Even less likely is the possibility that an actor plays this other actor once and then never plays a similar game with a like player again. Given the prevalence of repetition, we turn to the subject of repetition in this section and consider its effect on the manner in which the players participate in the game.

Let us return to the game presented in figure 1. This is an extensive form game in which the United States will always acquiesce and New Zealand will in turn rebel. This is also a game of complete and perfect information. We can expand this game to include other allies. This is done by having the United States play a series of allies that have the same payoff structure as does New Zealand.[18] The game in figure 1 then becomes a constituent game that is repeated or iterated. Will repetition change the equilibrium of this game?

If there is a finite number of allies facing the United States, the United States, surprisingly, will maximize its payoff by acquiescing. In each constituent part of the game, the United States gets a higher payoff by acquiescing than by punishing a rebellion. This fact prevents the United States from building a tough reputation at the beginning of the iterated game, which is then used to force the remaining allies to choose to acquiesce instead of punish. This result is developed using backwards induction. Take for example, a case in which the United States faces 17 allies sequentially (all playing a game identical to the one in figure 1). Given the same payoffs in the final period as in the first period, Player 17 maximizes her payoffs by rebelling; the United States' corresponding decision is to play cooperatively. Why does this occur? The United States has no incentive to punish the seventeenth ally given that this is the last stage of the game; it no longer needs to worry about its reputation. The seventeenth ally, realizing this fact, then chooses to rebel since no punishment will be forthcoming. Working backward along the tree, we can show that the same decisions hold for all periods of play. The United States would not punish a rebellion of the sixteenth ally since it knows that its actions will have no affect on the future actions of the seventeenth ally. The sixteenth ally would then choose to rebel since no punishment would be forthcoming. This process, which is called backwards induction, can be repeated for each constituent part of the game. What is rational in the last period is rational for all the periods. Thus, the United States would always choose to acquiesce and the allies would

18. If the payoffs of the players are the same and if each player is aware of the outcome of each game, it does not matter whether we are talking about the interaction between the United States and a series of other nations or the United States and New Zealand repeatedly interacting. Both games would be analyzed in the same fashion.

always choose to rebel. Repetition, then, does not assure the occurrence of reputation building. And, more importantly, it does not change the strategies that are being played in the constituent games of the repeated game. In both games, the United States chooses to acquiesce and New Zealand chooses to rebel.

How can repetition change the strategies played in this game or a similar one? There are two answers to this question. These answers are based on the potential number of repetitions of this game as well the level of information available to the players of the game. Changing the game from one of finite known repetitions to one with either infinite repetitions or an unknown stopping point changes the behavior of the actors in the game. For instance, the allies can no longer rely on backwards induction to solve this game. Instead, other techniques must be considered.

Shubik (1970), Taylor (1976, 1987) and Axelrod (1980a, 1980b, 1981, 1984) have all shown that cooperation can be sustained in a repeated Prisoners' Dilemma game under certain conditions. They show that when the game is played with the discounting of future payoffs and/or an exogenous probability of the game terminating after a finite number of iterations mutual cooperation can arise as one of the equilibria of the game. This finding is remarkable given that the only Nash equilibrium in this game in its single-shot form is defection. In its repeated form, there are many more equilibria.

Axelrod's *The Evolution of Cooperation* (1984) has had a significant impact on the use of game theory in political science, especially in the field of international relations. For example, Keohane's *After Hegemony: Cooperation and Discord in the World Political Economy* (1984) and a whole issue of *World Politics* (1985) are based upon Axelrod's findings. In Axelrod's formulation[19] of the repeated Prisoners' Dilemma, cooperation may or may not emerge depending on the importance each player places on future payoffs or, in other words, the manner in which they discount the utility of the outcomes of future actions. Before considering an application to our case study, we consider a problem with this approach concerning the number of possible equilibria.

In game theory, repeated games have been of interest for many years. This interest has resulted in a set of findings that have been commonly labeled "folk theorems." Ordeshook (1992) summarizes these theorems in the following manner.

---

19. This formulation is very similar to Taylor's work (1976, 1987).

In an infinitely repeated game, any outcome that gives each
player what that player can guarantee himself if he plays the
game without coordinating with anyone else—any outcome that
satisfies the security value of each player—can correspond to an
equilibrium.[20] (179–80)

This family of theorems leads us to the conclusion that there can be a
plethora of equilibria in an infinitely repeated game. For example, in
the Prisoners' Dilemma game presented in matrix 1 one can find an
equilibrium set of strategies for any outcome that would provide each
player at minimum his or her security value. In this case, each player
would need to average a payoff of at least 2 per round. There can exist
a large number of equilibria that support or provide such payoffs. Two
such strategies would be {All C, All C} and {All D, All D}. Of course,
there are more complicated strategies that would provide the same
payoffs. And, since an equilibrium is defined by its strategies and not
its payoffs, any of these could be an equilibrium.

How does the Folk Theorem affect our analysis of the interaction
between the United States and New Zealand? An easy answer would
be that it provides support for the actions of the United States and
New Zealand in an interaction as portrayed in figure 4. However, this
answer is problematic in two ways. First, we would need to find the
equilibrium strategy that would yield this payoff in a constituent game
of the repeated game. This would not be difficult. For example, {All
R, All P} would yield this payoff in each and every constituent game
of the repeated game. However, this strategy would not be an equilibrium because it does not provide both players' with their security
levels. New Zealand does get its security level, which is $-d$. The
United States, however, does not. It receives $-p$ where the security
level is 0.

The payoff for the United States does not necessarily lead us to
rule out the game in figure 4 as an incorrect representation of the
interaction between the United States and New Zealand. All we have
argued is that the {All R, All P} is not an equilibrium. We could still
have an equilibrium in which both parties receive their respective
payoffs of $-p$ and $-d$ in one round or many rounds. In fact, we could
have several equilibria in which these payoffs are received in one or

---

20. A security value is the lowest payoff a player can receive if she plays her "best"
strategy. For example, a security level for a player who has a dominant strategy would be
the worst payoff that strategy provides. Of course, one does not need a dominant strategy to
have a security level. The security level for the game in figure 2 is 1.

more interations of the game as long as the average payoff of the supergame is equal to or exceeds the security level for each player.

Thus, while repeated games do provide us with a way in solving this game in a "reasonable manner," that is, we find the solution that actually occurred, we are left with many other solutions. We do not have as yet a reasonable way to choose between these equilibria. As such, we are left with many equilibria in most repeated games.

Conclusion

In this chapter, we have taken the reader from very simple matrix games to games of incomplete information and repeated games. We have introduced simple concepts such as Nash equilibria and dominant strategies. We have also considered more complicated concepts such as subgame perfect equilibria, Bayesian equilibria, and the Folk Theorem. By now your head might be reeling from the amount of information that we have introduced in this chapter. Our purpose was not, however, to teach you all these concepts in such a short time. Instead, you will be seeing these concepts used in the next four chapters. This chapter merely introduced you to them. The next four chapters will serve to strengthen your knowledge by examining how they can be used to develop more fully the work of other political scientists.

CHAPTER 3

Strategic Choice and Progressive Ambition in American Politics: An Examination of Rohde's Model

Introduction

A common problem in political science is the usage of decision theory, implicitly or explicitly, to examine strategic interactions. Depending on the question being asked, using a decision theoretic focus may yield vastly different results than a game theoretic one will. By using decision theory instead of game theory to study political situations involving strategic interactions, scholars may ignore the importance of the strategic interactions between sets of actors.

For example, much of the literature on campaign donations by political action committees has focused on the committees' choices whom to provide with contributions. Scholars who focus on who gets how much money from political action committees usually consider only the characteristics of those receiving the money. These attributes include incumbency, seniority, committee membership, chairmanships of relevant committees, and commitment to the views supported by the political action committee. On the other hand, little work has been done concerning the ways in which choices by one political action committee affect and are affected by other political action committees. The strategic interaction part of this problem has not been addressed. Are conservative committees more or less likely to provide funds to a candidate running against a competitor who may receive substantial funds from liberal groups? Do liberal committees coordinate their spending in order to insure that most if not all liberal candidates are adequately funded? By focusing on the characteristics of the candidate and not the potential actions of other political action committees, these scholars may have missed part of the analysis.

Let us consider this problem more concretely. Each political action committee has a finite amount of money to divide between a finite number of candidates. For simplicity's sake assume that there are only two political action committees. One is liberal, and the other is conservative. There are six types of political candidates who possess combinations of two political characteristics, ideology and incumbency. These candidates are either liberal, moderate, or conservative, and they are either incumbents or challengers. How should the political action committees ration their resources? Clearly, the choice of any committee depends on what the other committee is doing. For example, if the liberal committee chooses to divide its funds evenly among liberal incumbents, the conservative committee may choose to provide token funding to conservative incumbents and use the rest of its money on moderate incumbents, moderate challengers, and conservative candidates who are challenging liberal incumbents. Given this strategy choice by the conservative committee, the liberal committee may choose to provide fewer funds to liberal incumbents and more funds to liberal challengers of conservative incumbents. Strategic considerations need to be considered in these situations.[1]

In this chapter, our focus is on another situation in which the strategic interaction between actors has not been taken into account. Rohde (1979) considers under what conditions incumbent officeholders will strive for higher office. Briefly, his theory argues that an incumbent will only try for higher office if the expected value of running for higher office is greater than the expectation of not running for higher office. His analysis is problematic because the potential actions of other actors, including other potential challengers and the incumbent in the higher office, are not explicitly taken into account. Actions of these other actors would surely have some effect on the incumbent's decision to pursue the higher office.

We focus on the problems that arise from modeling strategic situations using decision theory instead of game theory. In doing so, the differences between decision theory and game theory are noted. In addition, we explore the case studied by Rohde in order to illustrate why one should use game theory instead of decision theory to study a situation involving strategic interaction.

This chapter proceeds as follows. First, a brief introduction to decision theory is provided in which we contrast game theory with decision theory. Second, a more complete discussion of Rohde's model of progressive ambition is presented. In the discussion of his

---

1. Of course, one may object that this situation becomes too simplified by examining only two political action committees. Why is doing this to capture strategic interaction necessarily better than assuming n actors, treating $n - i$ as the environment for e and focusing on i's decisions? The answer to this question is "it depends." It depends on the question you are asking. The question, of course, frames the manner in which you approach the answer.

analysis, the problems with using decision theory in this and similar situations are noted. Third, we develop a set of simple game theoretic models in order to model explicitly the strategic interactions discussed in Rohde's analysis. Fourth, and finally, we consider the differences between mixed strategies and the decision theoretic techniques used in this chapter.

What Is Decision Theory?

Decision theory, unlike game theory, focuses on choices made by a single actor in which only his or her choice and nature can affect the outcome. A classic example from decision theory involves choosing between two lotteries. There are prizes offered in each lottery. Connected with each prize is a probability of winning that prize. Minimally, a lottery consists of a set of prizes and the probabilities of winning those prizes. These probabilities and payoffs are not affected by your action or the action of others.[2]

Figure 7 shows two simple lotteries. Which would you choose to play? In Lottery A, you have a 0.5 probability of winning $25.00 and a 0.5 probability of getting nothing. In Lottery B, you have a 0.4 probability of winning $36.00 and a 0.6 probability of getting nothing. Given this choice, most people would choose Lottery B over Lottery A. Why is that the case?

This would be the case if we believe a person making this choice uses expected utility calculations to make his or her decision. In this case, such a person would make the following calculation in which $E(\cdot)$ represents the expected value of a lottery:

$$E(A) = 0.5(25) + 0.5(0)$$
$$E(B) = 0.4(36) + 0.6(0).$$

The expected value of Lottery A is $12.50 while that of Lottery B is $14.40. A person who wants to maximize his or her expected payoff would choose Lottery B over Lottery A.

On a technical note, this decision holds if the person making this

---

2. Thus, a lottery in which people choose which number to play and the payoffs of the lottery are decided by the number of people playing and the number of people choosing the winning option would not be a lottery in the sense the term is used here. Instead, this lottery is similar to the scratch-off lotteries that have been adopted by a number of states. In these lotteries, all the cards are printed in advance. As such, the odds and payoffs are established in advance. When you buy your ticket you can easily find out the probability of getting certain payoffs.

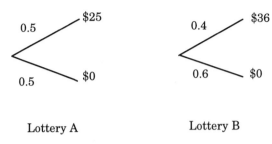

Fig. 7. **Choosing between two lotteries**

choice equates money with his or her utility. In other words, the above result is true if we assume that the person's utility function is linear in money. It will not hold for all types of utility functions. For example, assume that the person choosing between the two lotteries has a utility function that can be represented as

$$U(x) = \sqrt{x}.$$

The choice between lotteries then becomes

$$E(A) = 0.5(\sqrt{25}) + 0.5(\sqrt{0})$$
$$E(B) = 0.4(\sqrt{36}) + 0.6(\sqrt{0}).$$

This person would choose Lottery A since the expected value of A is 2.5 and that of B is 2.4.[3]

Decision theory, then, is used to describe situations in which a person is making a choice under risk. There is no strategic interaction between two or more players; rather, the player makes choices given her utility function, the possible outcomes, and the probabilities of these outcomes occurring. Decision theory differs from game theory, then, in two important aspects. First, a decision theoretic problem involves the calculations of only one player while a game theoretic problem involves the calculations of two or more players. Second, the actor in the decision theoretic problem takes an action that probabilistically leads to some outcome. The actor in a game theoretic

---

3. There are many different types of utility functions. For example, the utility function could be

$$U(x) = |x|.$$

problem takes an action that in combination with actions taken by other players yields an outcome.[4]

A Problem with Using Decision Theory to Model Strategic Interactions

A major problem with using decision theory to model a situation that is more suited to game theoretic analysis concerns the problem of interdependency. In a game theoretic situation, outcomes are arrived at by examining the intersection of the two players' strategies. In decision theory, outcomes are not seen as being dependent on the actions of others. When examining the former problem from the latter perspective, one can easily forget that the actions of others may be predicated on what they think your actions will be.[5] How could this affect the predicted versus the actual outcome of a game?

Matrix 8 illustrates a simple two-person game. Instead of analyzing it as a game, we first examine it from the perspective of decision theory. Player 1 would see this game as a choice between two lotteries. He could play lottery L or lottery R. If he chose to play L, he could expect one of two payoffs. He could receive 0 or 3. Assume that ω is the probability that he receives 0; then $1 - \omega$ is the probability that he receives 3. If he chose to play R, his payoffs would be 1 and 2 with the probability of ω and $1 - \omega$, respectively. The probabilities are identical between L and R because Player 1 assumes that his actions or potential actions will have no effect on Player 2's choices. In other words, he ignores any chance of strategic interaction in this situation. Thus, he creates the following set of expectations in which ω is the probability that Player 2 chooses L:

$$E(L) = \omega(0) + (1 - \omega)(3)$$

$$E(R) = \omega(1) + (1 - \omega)(2).$$

4. Of course, probability could still play a role in this situation. For example, a player could choose to use a mixed strategy. See chapter 2 for a brief discussion of mixed strategies.

5. Of course, in situations in which there are many actors, one may want to use decision theory instead of game theory. An example of this situation is a model of perfect competition in microeconomics. In this situation, individual firms see themselves as price takers, that is, their choice of price does not affect other competing firms. See chapter 4 for a discussion of using game theory versus decision theory in situations with many actors.

Player 2

		L	R
Player 1	L	0,2	3,3
	R	1,3	2,3

Matrix 8. A simple matrix game illustrating the interdependence of choices

Solving these equations simultaneously,[6] we find that Player 1 will choose L if the probability that Player 2 chooses L is less than one-half. Player 1 will choose R if the probability that Player 2 chooses L is greater than one-half. If these probabilities are equal, then Player 1 receives the same expected payoff regardless of his choice. Of course, the value of ω is subjective.

Player 2, of course, would be making similar calculations. She has a choice between two lotteries, L and R. If she chooses L, her payoff will be either 2 or 3. Assume that the probabilities of these payoffs will be α and $1 - \alpha$, respectively. If she chooses R, her payoff will be 3. The probability of this payoff is, of course, 1.[7] Player 2 would evaluate the following expectations in order to decide between these two lotteries.

---

6. To solve these two equations simultaneously, we first create the inequality

$E(L) > E(R)$.

We then replace the expectation operators to create the inequality

$\omega(0) + (1 - \omega)(3) > \omega(1) + (1 - \omega)(2)$.

This expression can be simplified as

$$3 - 3\omega > \omega + 2 - 2\omega$$
$$-3\omega > -\omega - 1$$
$$-2\omega > -1$$
$$\omega < \tfrac{1}{2}.$$

Thus, $E(L)$ is greater than $E(R)$ if $\omega < .5$.
7. This probability is 1 since $[\alpha + (1 - \alpha)] = 1$.

$$E(L) = \alpha(2) + (1 - \alpha)(3)$$

$$E(R) = \alpha(3) + (1 - \alpha)(3)$$

Solving these two equations simultaneously, one finds that Player 2 will always choose R unless α equals 0. At that probability, Player 2 is indifferent between R and L.

The joint solution of these decision theoretic problems is:

    a. If $\alpha = 0$, then Player 2 will be indifferent between L and R and
        i. If $\omega > 0.5$, then Player 1 will choose R.
        ii. If $\omega < 0.5$, then Player 1 will choose L.
        iii. If $\omega = 0.5$, then Player 1 will choose either R or L with equal probability.
    b. If $\alpha > 0$, then Player 2 will choose R and
        i. If $\omega > 0.5$, then Player 1 will choose R.
        ii. If $\omega < 0.5$, then Player 1 will choose L.
        iii. If $\omega = 0.5$, then Player 1 will choose either R or L.

All four outcomes are possible when players examine this situation from a decision theoretic perspective. The final outcome is dependent upon the subjective estimate by Player 1 of the probability of Player 2 playing one of her two strategies and the subjective estimate by Player 2 of Player 1 playing one of his two strategies. If α equals 0, then Player 2 will be indifferent between L and R. If $\alpha > 0$, then Player 2 will choose R. If ω is greater than 0.5, then Player 1 will choose R. If ω is less than 0.5, then Player 1 will choose L. It is possible, then, to have any of the four possible outcomes occur.

What would be the outcome if we analyzed this situation as a game? Player 2's strategy R weakly dominates strategy L. R weakly dominates L since Player 2 receives payoffs from this strategy that are not less than the payoffs yielded by L and, in some cases, are better than those payoffs. Given this domination, Player 1 is safe in assuming that Player 2 will play R regardless of what Player 1 does. Thus, Player 1 will choose to play L. Player 2, realizing that Player 1 will be reasoning in this manner, will in turn play R. The outcome of the game would then be $\{L,R\}$. This outcome is a Nash equilibrium.

Thus, different results occur when we analyze this situation in a decision theoretic manner rather than as a game. In the former case, there are two possible outcomes. Any of the four possible strategy combinations are possible if this situation is examined from a decision theoretic point of view. In the game theoretic situation, there is one determinate outcome, {L,R}.[8] Why would the other three outcomes not occur if both players analyzed the situation from a game theoretic perspective? For the outcomes {L,L} and {R,L} to occur, Player 2 would have to choose a strategy, L, which is weakly dominated by R. There is no incentive for her to make this choice since she will always do at least as well if not better than L by choosing R. Outcome {R,R} would only occur if Player 1 chose to ignore the fact that for Player 2 R weakly dominates L. Given this weak domination, Player 1 has no reason to expect that Player 2 would choose L. As long as that is the case his only real choice is that of R. From a game theoretic viewpoint, we may exclude {R,R} as a potential outcome since it would only result from one player believing that the other player is going to play a weakly dominated strategy.

Before proceeding to Rohde's model of progressive ambition, let us examine two simple situations and consider whether game theory or decision theory would be more useful in examining them. Candidates for political office take policy stances that they think will attract voters. The choice of stances involve both game theoretic and decision theoretic frameworks. Each candidate must decide what will appeal to potential voters. In examining possible policy stances, the candidate takes the voters as given and determines which stances will appeal to the most voters. Here the voters' preferences are assumed to be given and to respond to the candidates choices. At the same time, the candidate has to worry about the actions of other candidates. Their appeals may be more attractive to certain segments of the potential electorate. For example, a Republican candidate may try to moderate her stance by taking a pro-choice position. This might appeal to a large number of potential voters. However, when making this decision, she must consider whether a Democratic candidate may try to appeal to disaffected voters by taking a pro-life stance. Thus, the taking of positions by candidates for public office combines both a decision theoretic and a game theoretic focus. Appealing to voters could be effectively modeled using decision theory, while considering the choices of one's opponents would be more appropriately considered with game theory.

In this section, we have argued that approaching game theoretic

---

8. The reader should not assume that game theoretic approaches will always yield fewer outcomes than decision theoretic approaches do. It could easily be the case that the game theoretic approach would yield several outcomes or equilibria. The point of this example is to show that one's results differ depending on whether game theory or decision theory is used.

problems from a decision theoretic perspective can yield different results. Implicitly we have argued that results derived from the misapplication of decision theory will not occur when the situation is analyzed properly.

In the next section, Rohde's model of progressive ambition is introduced. This model was explicitly developed in a decision theoretic framework. After introducing this model, factors that might lead one to decide to model the same situation as a game are discussed.

Rohde's Model of Progressive Ambition

In Joseph Schlesinger's *Ambition and Politics: Political Careers in the United States* (1966, 9–10) three types of political ambition are discussed. These are discrete, static, and progressive. Discrete ambition applies to a politician who seeks an office for a specific length of time, usually one term, and then retires from political life. Static ambition applies to a politician who seeks and attains a political office with the purpose of holding that office as long as possible. A politician of this type does not try to move from this office to a higher one. Progressive ambition applies to a politician who holds an office *and* seeks to obtain an office that is considered to be of higher status. Jack Kemp and Richard Gephardt would both be considered politicians with progressive ambitions. These politicians, who either were or are members of the U.S. House of Representatives, were willing to try to move from their current positions to the White House.

While Schlesinger assumes that manifested behavior can be used as a proxy for what type of ambition a politician possesses, Rohde argues that almost all members of the House have progressive ambitions. He states the assumption that "if a member of the House, on his first day of service, were offered a Senate seat or a governorship *without cost or risk,* he would take it" (3). Static ambition, on the other hand, is only seen when the member for some reason is not able to pursue higher office. In other words, static ambition is manifested when the costs or risks of pursuing higher office are too high. Thus, Rohde's focus shifts from that of Schlesinger (categorizing politicians into different ambition types) to one of examining the conditions under which incumbents will choose to run for higher office.

To examine this decision by candidates, he develops the following decision calculus. The candidate chooses between a_1, in which she chooses to run for her currently held office (that is, reelection) and a_2, in which she chooses to pursue higher office. These cases are mutually exclusive. Thus, a politician who chooses to run for higher office must relinquish her present seat. $C(a_j)$ represents the direct utility cost incurred by choosing alternative j. These costs would include the cost of campaigning for the different offices. Each action can yield one of three outcomes. The politician will not occupy an office after the election (O_1), will hold her present office after the election (O_2), or will hold the higher office being considered after the election (O_3). These outcomes, of course, are also assumed to be mutually exclusive. $U(O_j)$ represents the utility the incumbent receives if outcome j occurs. Finally, the incumbent assigns a probability $P_i(O_j)$ that outcome j will occur if action i is taken. For example, the probability that the incumbent will win higher office if she chooses not to run for it is represented by $P_1(O_3)$. The first subscript refers to the action taken by the incumbent. In this case, the action is to run for reelection. The second subscript categorizes the type of outcome being examined. In this case, the outcome is the incumbent moving to higher office.

To understand an incumbent's choice of whether or not to run for higher office, Rohde examines the expectations

$$E(a_1) = P_1(O_1)U(O_1) + P_1(O_2)U(O_2) \\ + P_1(O_3)U(O_3) - C(a_1) \tag{3.1}$$

$$E(a_2) = P_2(O_1)U(O_1) + P_2(O_2)U(O_2) \\ + P_2(O_3)U(O_3) - C(a_2). \tag{3.2}$$

Rohde simplifies these expectations by assuming that a candidate can only run for one office at a time. Therefore, $P_1(O_3) = P_2(O_2) = 0$. In addition, he assumes that O_1 is the least preferred alternative. This seems reasonable for his purposes since he assumes that all politicians have progressive ambition. As such, the worst possible alternative for these politicians is that of holding no office. Since O_1 is the least preferred alternative, he arbitrarily sets $U(O_1) = 0$. This simplifies expectations (3.1) and (3.2) to

$$E(a_1) = P_1(O_2)U(O_2) - C(a_1) \tag{3.3}$$

$$E(a_2) = P_2(O_3)U(O_3) - C(a_2). \tag{3.4}$$

A run for higher office is justified if and only if

$$[P_2(O_3)U(O_3) - P_1(O_2)U(O_2)] - [C(a_2) - C(a_1)] > 0. \tag{3.5}$$

In other words, a run for higher office will be made if and only if the expected value of running for the office is greater than the expected value of not running for the office. If this were the only result from Rohde's model, this article would not have been cited and used by numerous authors.[9] Rohde presents seven hypotheses, which are developed using comparative statics arguments.

H_1: Among House members, the proportion of opportunities to run for the Senate that is taken will be greater than the proportion of opportunities taken to run for governor. (7–8)

H_2: Among House members, the proportion of opportunities to run for governorships with a four-year term that is taken will be greater than the proportion of opportunities taken to run for governorships with a two-year term. (8)

H_3: Among House members, for both Senate and gubernatorial races, the proportion of opportunities to run for higher office that is taken in situations where no incumbent is seeking reelection will be greater than the proportion of opportunities taken in situations where an incumbent is seeking reelection. (9)

H_4: Among House members, for both Senate and gubernatorial races, the proportion of opportunities to run for higher office that is taken in states which are "safe" for the opposition party will be less than the proportion of opportunities taken in states which are competitive or "safe" for their own party. (9)

H_5: Among House members, for Senate races, the probability that a House member will run will be directly related to the proportion of the state's population the population of his House constituency comprises. (11)

H_6: For both Senate and gubernatorial races, the probability that a House member will run will be inversely related to his seniority. (11–12)

H_7: If two House members are presented with similar opportunities to seek higher office, and one is a "risk taker" and the other is not, then the "risk taker" will have a greater probability of running for higher office than the other. (12)

Of these seven hypotheses, five of them clearly describe decision theoretic situations when all other factors are held constant. The re-

9. For example, see Hibbing 1982a, 1982b; Robeck 1982; Sapiro 1982; Brace 1984; Loomis 1984; Squire 1989, 1991; Copeland 1989; Canon and Sousa 1992; Abramson, Aldrich, and Rohde 1987; and Banks and Kiewiet 1989.

maining two hypotheses, the third and seventh, are game theoretic in nature and, as such, cannot be considered properly by means of Rohde's decision theoretic approach. Before discussing these two hypotheses, let us first examine why the remaining five hypotheses are decision theoretic in nature.

Three of these hypotheses, the first, second, and sixth, concern the value a candidate places on either her present office or the higher office. The first two hypotheses concern the length of term of a U.S. senator vis-à-vis a state governor. The first hypothesis is derived from the fact that no term of a state governor is longer than four years while that of a senator is six years. The second hypothesis differentiates between governorships with two-year versus four-year terms. In both of these hypotheses, it is argued that representatives will be more willing to take the risk of running for higher office as the length of term of such an office increases. The sixth hypothesis does not focus on the length of term of a candidate's potential office. Instead, it takes into account the fact that members of the House of Representatives gain more influence as their seniority grows. As such, as a member's seniority increases, the ratio of benefits of her present position vis-à-vis either a governorship or a Senate seat increases. The average member would be less likely to run for higher office as her seniority increases because she would not see a major increase in utility from such an exchange of offices. In each of these cases, a potential challenger cannot affect the utility of the position or the probability of gaining the position through her choice. A decision theoretic model would be appropriate in considering each of these three situations.

The other two hypotheses that are decision theoretic in nature are Hypotheses 4 and 5. These concern the probability of the member winning a contest for higher office. The fourth hypothesis concerns the disposition of voters in the state to elect candidates from her party. A potential candidate will be more likely to run if her party wins a disproportionate number of the offices in the state. The fifth hypothesis concerns the candidate's electoral base of her current office. As the proportion of this base increases relative to the electorate for higher office, the member is more likely to run for this higher office. Both of these hypotheses concern factors that the potential challenger does not directly control. Or, at minimum, she does not control these factors in the short run. Neither party identification nor geographic electoral base can be manipulated by potential candidates or the incumbent in the short run.[10]

---

10. Of course, there may be some form of manipulation occurring in the case of

While these five hypotheses clearly fall within the realm of decision theory, the other two do not. The third hypothesis concerns the likelihood of members running for higher office in situations in which there is no incumbent versus those in which there is an incumbent. Rohde conjectures that a member is more likely to run for higher office if there is no incumbent running for reelection to that office. While on the surface this case seems to be one in which decision theory is applicable, this is not the case. The choice of the incumbent may be based on that of a potential challenger. For example, when Governor Charles S. Robb of Virginia was contemplating a run for the Senate, the incumbent Republican, Paul S. Trible Jr., decided not to run for reelection. Though Trible stated publicly that he had decided not to run for reelection because of his inability to make good public policy in Washington, it was widely assumed that his action occurred because he believed Robb would run for his seat and win. In this case, clearly the incumbent chose to give up his seat because of a potential challenger. How does this affect Rohde's hypothesis?

The problem with Hypothesis 3 is that it assumes that the action of the potential challenger has no effect on the incumbent. This is clearly not the case. Both the incumbent and the potential challenger are dealing with a case of strategic choice or interdependent decision making. These situations should be considered by using game theory not decision theory. In other words, it is important in this situation to take into account the potential actions of the incumbent as well as those of the challenger.

Finally, we move to examine Rohde's seventh hypothesis. In this hypothesis, Rohde considers how potential candidates consider risk as a reason for them to run or not run for higher office. This leads him to divide the population into two parts: people who are risk takers and people who are risk averse. The second person choosing between two lotteries earlier in this chapter illustrates the case of a risk taker. In this example, the person is willing to take the riskier alternative, that is, the one with a higher probability of winning nothing, because he or she valued the higher payoff in that lottery much more than the highest payoff in the other lottery.[11] The first person choosing between the two lotteries is an example of someone who is risk neutral. Rohde argues that potential candidates who are risk acceptant are more likely

---

Hypothesis 4, that is, a potential candidate may choose to switch parties. See Aldrich and Bianco 1991 for a discussion of this topic.

11. For a discussion of risk acceptance, risk averseness, and risk neutrality, see Ordeshook 1986.

to run for higher office, given similar situations, than are those who are risk averse.

While this argument is fundamentally a decision theoretic argument, the problem that arises in Rohde's analysis is his operationalization of this variable. He categorizes a member as a risk taker if the member originally ran for his House seat when an incumbent was running for reelection or if the other party received 57 percent or more of the vote during the last three previous elections. If a potential challenger did not satisfy either of these requirements, they were labeled as "other."[12]

Why is this definition problematic? It is problematic for the same reasons that Rohde's third hypothesis was challenged. The decision of an incumbent to retire may be predicated on the actions of the potential challenger. However, a candidate may be classified as "other" if she happens to run against an incumbent who chooses to retire instead of facing certain defeat at the hands of the challenger. For example, would we consider Senator Robb of Virginia to be "other" because the incumbent declined to run against him for this office? In this case, the potential candidate's actions have affected those of the incumbent. Strategic interaction does take place. This situation is game theoretic because the actions of one of the actors are predicated on the potential actions of the other candidate.

In the next section, we explore these topics further. Two simple game theoretic models are developed, which consider the strategic nature for both actors of whether or not to run for office. In analyzing these games, we show that the results of the model will change depending on whether the incumbent and the potential challenger view the situation as being game theoretic or decision theoretic. The reader should note that these games do not capture the entire essence of the situation. A more complicated model will be considered in the sixth chapter of this book. This more complicated model is not presented here because it uses a game of incomplete information. This type of game will be considered more completely in chapter 5.

Explicitly Considering the Strategic Aspects of Progressive Ambition

In this section, two models are developed concerning the choices of both an incumbent and a potential challenger to run for office. The first model examines a situation in which the incumbent has the upper

12. To be fair to Rohde, it should be noted that he argues that this group of "others" should be considered "[n]ot as 'risk averters' because we do not know that they would not

hand, that is, he will win the upcoming election regardless of whether the potential challenger decides to enter the race. In this case, it is shown that by approaching this problem from a decision theoretic standpoint the potential challenger may make the wrong decision, entering even though she has no hope of winning the race. The second model considers a case in which the incumbent will lose if the potential challenger actually enters the race. Once again, it is demonstrated that an incumbent using a decision theoretic approach may actually decide not to retire even though he will be defeated by the challenger. Each of these cases are similar to those considered in Rohde's hypotheses 3 and 7. These models illustrate that problems occur when one analyzes game theoretic situations using decision theory.[13]

Matrix 9 illustrates a simple electoral game between an incumbent and a challenger. The incumbent has two strategies. He can decide to either pursue reelection, R, or leave office, L. The challenger also has two strategies. She can either enter the campaign for higher office, E, or stay with her present office, S. The payoffs for both actors are similar. The best outcome for each is attaining the elected office held by the incumbent; this payoff is presented as 1. The second best outcome is not to run an unsuccessful campaign; this payoff is presented as 0. The worst outcome is to wage an unsuccessful campaign. This payoff is represented by -1. Matrix 9 presents a game in which the incumbent is electorally invulnerable to the challenger, that is, the incumbent is returned to office regardless of whether the challenger decides to run. In this case, the incumbent has a dominant strategy of vying for reelection. One would then expect the incumbent to choose this strategy when playing this game. The challenger, however, does not have a dominant strategy. The lack of a dominant strategy in this case does not lead to any indeterminacy of outcomes.[14] This is caused by the fact that the challenger knows that the incumbent has a dominant strategy. As such, the challenger has no reason to believe that the incumbent will play any strategy but R. The outcome (and equilibrium) of this game is then $\{S,R\}$.

Of course, this outcome assumes that both players view this situation as one in which there is strategic interaction between both

have run if the previous incumbent had run" (1979, 15, n. 27). Rohde's emphasis on this claim actually strengthens our case because it illustrates the strategic nature of the interaction between the incumbent and any potential candidate.

13. Of course, a more complete model would include a set of potential challengers instead of a single challenger. However, N-person games are not considered until the next chapter. Thus, here we will only consider the two-candidate case.

14. See chapter 2 concerning situations in which multiple equilibria exist.

Incumbent

	R	L
E	-1,1	1,0
S	0,1	0,0

Challenger

Matrix 9. A simple matrix game with a strong incumbent

actors. What happens if one of the actors instead sees this case as decision theoretic in nature? Assume that the payoffs of the game remain the same, but the challenger believes that he is playing a game against Nature. If he approaches his choice from a decision theoretic vantage point, he must choose between the following two lotteries, in which α is the probability that the incumbent will not retire and $0 \leq \alpha \leq 1$:

$$E_c(E) = \alpha(-1) + (1 - \alpha)(1) \tag{3.6}$$

$$E_c(S) = \alpha(0) + (1 - \alpha)(0). \tag{3.7}$$

After simplifying these equations, we find that E is preferred to S if the challenger believes that the probability that the incumbent will run again is less than one-half. The challenger then will enter the race if and only if she perceives this probability to be less than 0.5. This result, of course, is different from what would happen if both players were examining this situation from a game theoretic standpoint. Thus, a potential challenger may find herself pursuing a hopeless challenge because she chose to use decision theory instead of game theory.

What if the situation is not hopeless for the challenger? Matrix 10 illustrates a case in which the challenger now has a dominant strategy. In this case, the challenger wins the higher office regardless of whether the incumbent decides to run. The equilibrium of this game, then, is {E,L}. The challenger plays her dominant strategy, E, and the incumbent, noting that choice, chooses to leave office, L.

This outcome once again assumes that both players are looking upon this situation as game theoretic. What if the incumbent decided to approach this problem from a decision theoretic standpoint instead? In this case, the incumbent would be choosing between the following

Incumbent

	R	L
E	1,−1	1,0
S	0,1	0,0

Challenger

Matrix 10. A simple matrix game with a strong challenger

two lotteries, in which β represents the probability that the challenger chooses not to run for higher office and $0 \leq \beta \leq 1$:

$$E_I(R) = \beta(1) + (1 - \beta)(-1) \tag{3.8}$$

$$E_I(L) = \beta(0) + (1 - \beta)(0). \tag{3.9}$$

After simplifying these two lotteries, we find that the incumbent will choose to run for reelection if he perceives that the probability of the challenger running is less than 0.5. Thus, once again a different result occurs depending on whether one uses game or decision theory. In this case, an incumbent with no chance of retaining his office may choose to run again if he misperceives the probability of a challenger running against him. This misperception occurs because he fails to realize that the challenger is not choosing between two lotteries.

How does this analysis affect Rohde's hypotheses and/or results? Since only the third and the seventh hypotheses improperly had a decision theoretic focus, our consideration is limited to those hypotheses. By examining the simple models developed above, it is clear that both of these hypotheses are affected when they are considered from a game theoretic instead of a decision theoretic perspective. In the third hypothesis, Rohde posits that members of the House will be more likely to run for open seats than for those held by incumbents who are seeking reelection. Our analysis illustrates that incumbents may choose to leave office because of a potential challenge. Of course, if the incumbent chooses not to run for reelection, the race becomes one for an open seat. Rohde would then use this race as a case to provide support for this hypothesis. However, the incumbent stepped down because of a potential challenge. The challenger, then, did not decide to run because the seat was open. In fact, the challenger caused the seat to become open. Thus, our simple models lead us to question Rohde's results concerning his third hypothesis.

On the other hand, our models lead to the opposite conclusion about the seventh hypothesis. This hypothesis concerns the actions of risk takers vis-à-vis those who were classified as "others." Here our original problem dealt not with the hypothesis but with the way in which the notion of risk taker is operationalized. For a person to be a risk taker, she needed either to have run for her House seat against an incumbent or to have run for an open House seat in a district in which the other party in the prior three elections received on average at least 57 percent of the total vote. In this case, Rohde's coding of the data may have understated his case. This would occur if the incumbent in the House seat chose not to run for reelection because of his potential challenger. The challenger may or may not be a risk taker. We cannot garner any evidence about the challenger in this situation based on the actions of the incumbent. In any event, Rohde may have under-counted the number of risk takers in his data set.

In this section, we demonstrated how one could get misleading results in the case of progressive ambition if one used decision theory instead of game theory. We also showed how Rohde's hypotheses are affected by examining them in game theoretic instead of decision theory terms. In the next section, we briefly consider the role of mixed strategies in game theory. Specifically, we show how mixed strategies are different from a decision theoretic approach.

A Comment on Mixed Strategies and Decision Theory

In chapter 2, we introduced mixed strategies. A mixed strategy is the result of a player deciding to choose between two or more strategies in a random fashion. In this section, we address how mixed strategies differ from the decision theoretic techniques examined in this chapter.

Matrix 11 presents a game of Chicken. In this game, neither player has a dominant strategy. In chapter 2, we showed that there are three Nash equilibria to this game. Two are pure strategy Nash equilibria. These are $\{R,L\}$ and $\{L,R\}$. There is also a mixed strategy equilibrium to this game. This is $\{(0.5,0.5),(0.5,0.5)\}$.

What does this mixed strategy Nash equilibrium mean? We can interpret it as Player 1 randomly choosing between L and R with a probability of 0.5. Player 2 would choose in a similar manner.

Why is this strategy combination a Nash equilibrium? It is an equilibrium because no single actor has an incentive to deviate given the action of the other player. For example, assume that Player 1

		Player 2	
		L	*R*
Player 1	*L*	0,0	3,1
	R	1,3	2,2

Matrix 11. A matrix game representation of Chicken

continues to play this mixed strategy, but Player 2 decides to deviate by playing either of the pure stategies. If Player 2 plays her pure strategy *R*, her expected payoff is 1.5; if she plays her pure strategy *L*, her expected payoff is also 1.5. For the mixed strategy combination to be a Nash equilibrium, the expected payoff must be at least as high as 1.5. The expected payoff of the mixed strategy equilibrium is also 1.5. Since this is a symmetric game, neither player has an incentive to change strategies. In this game, there are three possible strategy combinations in equilibrium. These are the two pure strategies and the one mixed strategy.

From a decision theoretic perspective, the following outcomes are possible. Player 1 chooses *L* if the probability of Player 2 playing *L* is less than 0.5. If the probability that Player 2 will play *L* is greater than 0.5, then Player 1 chooses *R*. Since this is a symmetric game, these same conditions hold for Player 2's choices given her beliefs about the probability of *R* and *L* occurring. Using this perspective, any of the four outcomes could occur depending on the subjective probability estimates of the two players.

How are probabilities used in these two cases? In a mixed strategy, a probability is found that maximizes the payoff of the player subject to the actions of the other player. For this mixed strategy to be part of an equilibrium, neither player should have an incentive to deviate from the mixed strategy. On the other hand, the probabilities used in the decision theoretic calculus are subjective estimates. Each player decides independently what action to take given his or her subjective estimate of the probability that certain events will occur. They do not let the effects of their calculation on the other player be taken into account.

For example, what if in the game theoretic analysis of the Chicken game in matrix 11 one player decides to play a mixed strategy of (0.4,0.6)? Would such a strategy yield an equilibrium if the other player is playing (0.5,0.5)? In other words, do players have a reason to unilaterally change their strategies given this strategy pair? The second player does. This is shown below. Assume Player 1 has chosen the mixed strategy of (0.4,0.6). Can Player 2 get a better payoff than the 1.7 that would result from playing the mixed strategy (0.5,0.5)? Player 2 would have to maximize the following statement, in which α is the probability that she plays L:

$$\alpha[0.4(0) + 0.6(3)] + (1 - \alpha)[0.4(1) + 0.6(2)].$$

This expression reduces to

$$\alpha(1.8) + (1 - \alpha)(1.6).$$

This expression is maximized by setting α equal to 1. Player 2 would choose to play the pure strategy L instead of the mixed strategy (0.5,0.5). Thus, a change in the probabilities in one player's mixed strategy results in a different outcome.[15]

In a decision theoretic framework, a change in the probability estimates of the other party would not affect the players' actions. For example, if Player 2 changed her estimate of the probability of Player 1 choosing R, this would only affect her choice of action. There is no way it can affect Player 1's decision calculus. This is because the two players are not considering the strategic interaction between the two parties. A mixed strategy, then, explicitly takes into account the choices of the other players. On the other hand, a decision theoretic framework does not make these connections between players.

Conclusion

In this chapter, we have presented a case for why one should not use decision theory in situations that are clearly game theoretic. It has been argued that different results would be predicted depending on which method one was to use. We provided examples of this difference both abstractly and by examining Rohde's theory of risk takers. In our analysis of Rohde's hypotheses, our move to game theory yielded mixed results. With respect to one hypothesis, Rohde's decision theoretic framework overstated his case; in the other, it actually understated the case.

---

15. If Player 2 moved to R, Player 1 would react by abandoning his mixed strategy and choosing L. Of course, $\{L,R\}$ is one of the two mixed Nash equilibria.

The goal of this chapter, however, was not to criticize his work. Our goals were to show that (1) one gets different results if decision theory is used to examine a situation of strategic interdependence instead of game theory; and (2) the results yielded by the game theoretic approach in these situations are more reasonable. Did we satisfy these goals? Our results do vary from those derived from Rohde's decision theoretic focus. Thus, condition number one is met. However, little support for goal number two has been given. This results not from the appropriateness of the technique as much as from the operationalization of the variables.

The reader should note that the models presented in this chapter are very simplistic. For instance, how likely is it that the players in this game will move simultaneously or that they will know with certainty who will win the election? These topics will be addressed in the next two chapters. Chapter 4 considers the problem of simultaneous versus sequential moves while chapter 5 addresses the question of incomplete information. After presenting that material, we will revisit this problem of electoral risk bearing with a more complete model in chapter 6. In developing this model, we will also show how Rohde's hypotheses are consistent with it.

CHAPTER 4

Dynamic Games and the Politics
of International Trade: An Examination
# of Conybeare's *Trade Wars*

Introduction

In this chapter we examine how game theory has been applied to the
analysis of trade wars. Continuing with the theme of our book, we
emphasize how game theoretic models can be used to model political
phenomena with parsimony. John Conybeare has written an intriguing
book entitled *Trade Wars* (1987)[1] which analyzes issues of international trade. Expanding his analysis, we show how topics that he
addressed but did not explicitly model can be modeled directly. Conybeare often relies on factors not related to the games he has developed
to explain the strategic interactions between nations engaged in trade
conflict. He frequently turns to non–game theoretic solutions to answer the substantive questions he asks. We show how these explanations can be reached completely within the context of a game theoretic
framework. In no way do we take issue with the substantive conclusions presented in this fascinating book. Rather, we mean to extend
Conybeare's rich analysis and provide an introduction to a variety of
game theoretic modeling techniques.

This chapter consists of two parts. In the first we look at dynamic
games as opposed to static games. How do players move within a
game? Does it make a difference whether players move simultaneously or sequentially? If the moves are sequential, how does order of
choice affect outcomes? What happens if the game is repeated? The
second part of the chapter examines N-player games. How do N-
player games compare with two-player games? We answer these questions by focusing on the strategic aspects of trade policy.

Conybeare's Analysis of International Trade

Conybeare analyzes one of the most salient issues in political economy, conflict and cooperation over international trade. Lobbying pres-

---

1. The full title is *Trade Wars: The Theory and Practice of International Commercial Rivalry* (1987).

sure against free trade seems to be growing annually. The practice of economic brinkmanship is now so widespread that the future of institutions such as General Agreement on Tariffs and Trade (GATT) are called into question. Yet, we also have seen the evolution of the European Union (EU) and the creation of the North American Free Trade Agreement (NAFTA), which seem to demonstrate that cooperation is still possible. What are the prospects for international economic policy coordination? To answer this question, Conybeare examines the total breakdown of economic cooperation, trade war. One of Conybeare's fundamental assumptions is that trade wars are the product of strategic interactions between countries. His primary analytical emphasis is on bilateral conflict. This bilateral focus allows Conybeare to move from traditional microeconomic models of international trade to strategic games. The central difference between traditional models of international trade and game theoretic models of trade conflict revolves around the assumptions of perfectly competitive markets in which countries must be price takers. Microeconomic models of trade decisions in such an environment possess the characteristics of decision theory. The essential assumption of such models is that one country's actions do not affect others. Offering an alternative perspective, Conybeare models situations in which countries strategically interact. Game theory is most appropriate for the analysis of how nations strategically choose their trade policy. In this way, chapter 3 of our book echoes one of Conybeare's central points: trade wars are inherently strategic and are most appropriately modeled as games.

The central feature distinguishing each of his games is nation size. By size, Conybeare is specifically referring to import price elasticities in respective countries. Large countries face relatively higher import price elasticities while small countries are more at the mercy of the (international) market, facing low import price elasticities. While the correlation between size, as defined in terms of national income ratios and import price elasticity, is far from perfect, it is high. Size is directly related to the game structure through the determination of the payoffs. Conybeare operationalizes payoffs as products of revenue and balance of trade as affected by import price elasticities. We utilize this basic framework throughout this chapter. We differ with Conybeare when he draws on non–game theoretic explanations (cognitive aspects of bargaining, political linkages, and domestic politics) to address perceived model specification problems associated with his games. Our principal argument is that Conybeare does not have to rely on these extra–game theoretic concepts. By drawing on more sophisticated game theoretic modeling techniques we can address most of the problems and inconsistencies that so trouble Conybeare. We have the technology. We can build it. We can develop consistent, parsimonious models based on a consistent set of assumptions and analytical techniques.

Conybeare, reflecting most of the discipline of political science, focuses his game theoretic analysis on the use of several 2×2 strategic (matrix) form games, including Prisoners' Dilemma, Chicken, Stag Hunt, and Deadlock.[2] Chapter 2 provides a careful and detailed presentation of the structure and equilibria of these types of games. In this chapter we focus on how these games are applied to a political situation, international trade conflict. After presenting Conybeare's analysis, we reexamine international trade and conflict through the use of extensive form games and N-person games.

Conybeare draws on the Prisoners' Dilemma, Chicken, Deadlock, and Stag Hunt games to model aspects of trade cooperation and conflict. As applied to bilateral trade conflicts, these three two-player games involve two states (X,Y) which choose to either cooperate $(C,$ not to impose a tariff) or defect $(D,$ to impose a tariff). Arranged in a matrix, these choices of strategies produce four possible outcomes: $C_XC_Y, D_XD_Y, C_XD_Y, C_YD_X$. The general form of this game is presented in matrix 12. Arranging these payoffs ordinally defines these four games. Prisoners' Dilemma (matrix 13) is defined by an ordinal ranking for nation-state X of $D_XC_Y > C_XC_Y > D_XD_Y > C_XD_Y$. The Chicken game (matrix 14) is defined by an ordinal ranking for player X of $D_XC_Y > C_XC_Y > C_XD_Y > D_XD_Y$, where mutual defection leads to a disastrous outcome for both players. Stag Hunt (matrix 15) is defined by $C_XC_Y > D_XC_Y > D_XD_Y > C_XD_Y$ as arranged ordinally for country X, where one would expect to see mutual cooperation as long as players possess complete information and this payoff ordering does not change. Deadlock (matrix 16) occurs when $D_XC_Y > D_XD_Y > C_XC_Y > C_XD_Y$. The dominant strategy here, as with the Prisoners' Dilemma, is defection. This, in turn, leads to a mutual defection equilibrium, but one in which the outcome provides all players with a higher payoff than does mutual cooperation.

As was discussed in chapter 2, the equilibrium for the Prisoners' Dilemma game is mutual defection. While both players get higher payoffs from mutual cooperation than from mutual defection, there is no incentive for either player unilaterally to alter his or her choice from mutual defection. The game of Chicken, in which mutual defec-

2. For example, a whole issue of *World Politics* (1985) focused on the applications of Prisoners' Dilemma in international relations. Our book aims to broaden the set of game theoretic tools used in political science.

		Y: Cooperate	Y: Defect
X	Cooperate	C_X,C_Y	C_X,D_Y
	Defect	D_X,C_Y	D_X,D_Y

Matrix 12. The general form of the two-player, simultaneous move game

tion is least preferred, is characterized by two pure-strategy equilibria {cooperate, defect} and {defect, cooperate}, and a mixed strategy equilibrium.[3] Stag Hunt, on the other hand, possesses an equilibrium of mutual cooperation.

Each of these games are two-player, single-shot games with simultaneous moves. Actually, these games do not have to involve simultaneous play as long as each player does not know how another player has moved. We characterize games in which a player must make a move without knowing the full history of the game as contests of complete and imperfect information. Recall from chapter 2, perfect information means that all players know the full history of the game when they make their choices. Any game with simultaneous choice requires the players to make a decision without knowing how the other player has moved and is therefore a game of imperfect information. Such games of complete and imperfect information take the following form.

1. Players X and Y simultaneously select actions. Player X chooses a_X from the feasible set of A_X while Y chooses a_Y from the feasible set A_Y.
2. Payoffs are $u_X(a_X, a_Y)$ and $u_Y(a_X, a_Y)$.

The emphasis now is on imperfect information and the requirement that players must make decisions without knowing how other players have moved. As is evident in the preceding discussion, as payoffs vary across these different two-player, one-shot games, the equilibria change.

Using this game theoretic framework, Conybeare (1987, 44–45)

3. Please refer to our discussion of mixed strategy equilibria in chapter 2.

Y

	Cooperate	Defect
Cooperate	3,3	1,4
Defect	4,1	2,2

X

Matrix 13. Prisoners' Dilemma

derives three hypotheses regarding bilateral trade wars. These hypotheses involve games between two large countries, two small countries, and asymmetric conflict between a large and a small country.

1. In a trade conflict between two large countries, the payoff ordering reflects a Prisoners' Dilemma game. Given this game structure, each country has a dominant strategy to defect. These strategic choices lead to an equilibrium of mutual defection, an outcome that provides lower payoffs for both players than does mutual cooperation.[4]
2. Two small countries in a trade conflict face a game with a payoff ordering that combines the games of Chicken and Stag Hunt. The payoffs are ordered from best to worst, from mutual cooperation $(C_X C_Y)$, to unilateral defection $(D_X C_Y)$, to unilateral cooperation $(C_X D_Y)$, to mutual defection $(D_X D_Y)$. Cooperation here is the dominant strategy for both players, leading to an equilibrium of mutual cooperation in the Hybrid Chicken–Stag Hunt game.
3. Asymmetric conflict between a large and small country is defined by the small country facing a payoff ordering resembling the Hybrid Chicken–Stag Hunt game played between two small countries while the large country plays Deadlock. This asymmetric trade conflict game is characterized by an equilibrium of unilateral cooperation by the small country $(C_X D_Y)$ in which the small country is X and the large country is Y.

Let us examine each of these games played between two players involving single play with imperfect information. Subsequently we

---

Y

	Cooperate	Defect
Cooperate	3,3	2,4
Defect	4,2	1,1

X

Matrix 14. Chicken

examine each of these games under finitely repeated, infinitely repeated, sequential choice (perfect and complete information), and N-player conditions. The one-shot Prisoners' Dilemma is described above. Matrix 17 portrays the game played between two small countries, the hybrid Chicken–Stag Hunt game. The matrix demonstrates the propensity for a mutual cooperation outcome of this game. In light of this game we do not expect to see trade wars emerge between two small countries. This game addresses bilateral trade conflict between two countries of relatively equal size.

Conybeare also discusses asymmetric conflict that can take place between large and small countries. In such a situation, small countries (X) face a payoff ordering of $C_X C_Y > D_X C_Y > C_X D_Y > D_X D_Y$, while a large country's (Y's) preference ordering for payoffs is $D_Y C_X > D_Y D_X > C_Y C_X > C_Y D_X$. In such a situation, a small country only hurts itself by implementing a tariff. It cannot alter its terms of trade. The large country, on the other hand, unconditionally prefers defection, regardless of what the small country does. As a result of these preferences, $D_Y C_X$ (large country defects, small country cooperates) is the ex-

Y

	Cooperate	Defect
Cooperate	4,4	1,3
Defect	3,1	2,2

X

Matrix 15. Stag Hunt

		Y	
		Cooperate	Defect
X	Cooperate	2,2	1,4
	Defect	4,1	3,3

Matrix 16. Deadlock

pected result. This asymmetric game is portrayed in matrix 18. In the environment of these two-player simultaneous choice (imperfect information) games, we can expect trade wars between two large countries, no trade conflict between two small countries, and exploitation of a small country by a large country.

What substantive conclusions can be drawn from Conybeare's analysis? Under game theoretic conditions of single play with complete and imperfect information we can assess each hypothesis in turn. Regarding Hypothesis 1, big countries will fight trade wars. The characteristics of the Prisoners' Dilemma game make mutual defection the equilibrium. Hypothesis 2 points to the opposite conclusion for two small countries. The equilibrium for the Hybrid Chicken–Stag Hunt game is mutual cooperation with single play and imperfect information. Hypothesis 3 involves an Asymmetric Trade game between a large and small country. In this situation, the large country's dominant strategy to defect forces a small country to acquiesce. These conclusions stand under the game theoretic conditions of two-player, single-play games with imperfect and complete information. Conybeare's

		Y	
		Cooperate	Defect
X	Cooperate	4,4	2,3
	Defect	3,2	1,1

Matrix 17. Hybrid Chicken–Stag Hunt

Y

	Cooperate	Defect
Cooperate	4,2	2,4
Defect	3,1	1,3

X

Matrix 18. Asymmetric Trade

formal analysis is limited to these conditions. In the subsequent sections of this chapter, we examine Conybeare's three hypotheses in light of different game theoretic conditions. We first relax the single-play condition and examine repeated games.

Dynamic Games of Trade

Repeated Games of Trade

In the spirit of this book, Conybeare finds these simple models inadequate for explaining trade conflict. He extends his analysis by examining how these game structures are affected by iteration. In other words, how are one-shot and repeated games different? Making reference to a variety of works, Conybeare posits that iteration increases the prospects for mutual cooperation (free trade) for Prisoners' Dilemma, Stag Hunt, and Chicken.[5] We can reasonably assume that economic interactions cannot be restricted to single plays; such games are almost always ongoing, repeated over long periods of time. Repeated games thus provide a more accurate modeling base for modeling trade wars. Let us further examine Conybeare's insight. Does iteration allow mutual cooperation to be achieved more easily?

Finitely Repeated Games

What happens if these games are repeated finitely? If you know you will face a player again in the future, do you alter your behavior? How

---

5. Actually, Stag Hunt should produce mutual cooperation in either a one-shot or a repeated game environment.

are repeated games different from single-shot games? In this section we restrict our attention to two-period games. Suppose two nations play the imperfect information (simultaneous play) game twice, moving in the second round knowing what happened in the first round. Such a game is referred to as a two-stage game of complete but imperfect information. Consider the two-period Prisoners' Dilemma game. To solve this game, we work backward from stage 2 to stage 1. The equilibrium at the second stage of this game is the same as that of any other Prisoners' Dilemma game, mutual defection. This equilibrium holds regardless of the outcome of the first round. As a result, the first stage of the two-period Prisoners' Dilemma game resembles a one-shot game. Thus, the outcome of the two-stage Prisoners' Dilemma game is $D_X D_Y$ in the first stage and $D_X D_Y$ in the second stage. In fact, the outcome is mutual defection throughout.

The one-shot equilibrium holds across finitely repeated games generally as long as the game possesses a unique Nash equilibrium. The basic form of a finitely repeated game with complete and imperfect information (a game with simultaneous moves) takes the following form.

1. Players X and Y simultaneously select actions. Player X chooses a_{X_1} from the feasible set of A_{X_1} while Y chooses a_{Y_1} from the feasible set A_{Y_1}.
2. Players X and Y observe a_{X_1} and a_{Y_1} from stage one of the game and then simultaneously select actions a_{X_2} and a_{Y_2} from the feasible sets A_{X_2} and A_{X_2}.
3. Payoffs are $u_X(a_{X_1}, a_{Y_1})$ and $u_Y(a_{X_1}, a_{Y_1})$ for one stage of the game. Payoffs for the game are the sum of payoffs from each stage of the game.

If a unique Nash equilibrium holds for the single-shot version of a game, it will hold for all stages of a finitely repeated game. The principle that worked for the two-stage Prisoners' Dilemma game holds across other games with a single equilibrium.[6] Given that the payoffs for the game are the sum of all stages of the game, a single equilibrium that holds for one stage applies to the finitely repeated game for all stages.

---

6. This condition does not hold for games with more than one equilibrium. Take, for example, the game of Chicken. Repeat Chicken for two rounds and nine equilibria are possible. These equilibria are the possible combinations of (*cooperate*, *defect*), (*defect*, *cooperate*), and the game's mixed strategy equilibrium.

What are the implications of finitely repeating the games presented by Conybeare? All three of these games, Prisoners' Dilemma,
Hybrid Chicken–Stag Hunt, and Asymmetric Trade, possess unique
equilibria. Repeating these games a finite number of times does not
alter the outcome; the equilibria remain unchanged.

In his discussion of the Asymmetric Trade game, Conybeare
makes reference to a small country credibly threatening to hurt itself in order to induce a big country to cooperate. A paradox arises
similar to that of the Chain Store paradox.[7] The Chain Store paradox
derives from Selten's Chain Store game in which a chain store faces
potential competitors in several different towns who must decide
whether or not to enter the market. In turn, the chain store must decide
whether or not to engage in a price war with any entrant. For a single
round of the game the utility maximizing choice for the chain store is
to acquiesce and not engage in a price war intended to drive the
entrant out of business. The equilibrium set of strategies is {enter,
acquiesce}. The paradox is that if the game is repeated finitely the
chain store would be better off having deterred subsequent market
entry by driving early entrants out of business. The paradox involves
the apparent conflict that seems to emerge between short-run and
long-run self-interest.[8] In terms of the Asymmetric Trade game, this
short-term/long-term paradox revolves around a small country's attempt to establish a credible threat. In the short run the small country
is better off unilaterally cooperating, allowing the large country to
exploit the situation. In the long run the small country would be better
off convincing the large country that it is willing hurt itself to insure
cooperation. For the time being, however, the result of the finitely
repeated game holds; the equilibria for the finitely repeated Asymmetric Trade game is unilateral cooperation by the small country.

How do Conybeare's hypotheses fare under these game theoretic
conditions? Examining these hypotheses with two-player, finite play
games with complete and imperfect information, we see Conybeare's
conclusions unaffected. Each of the games associated with hypotheses
1, 2, and 3 possess a single equilibrium in the single play. Given these
unique equilibria the finitely repeated versions of these games possess
the same equilibria as do the single-play games.

---

7. See Selten 1978.
8. The problem with this paradox is that it is an artifact of the game structure.
Incomplete information games (to be discussed in the next chapter) better address these
issues. We will elaborate on this discussion in the sections of this chapter concerned with
sequential choice games and N-player games.

Infinitely Repeated Games

We have seen what happens when a game is repeated finitely. What happens when there is no clear end to a game? International economic relations such as trade should be considered to be infinitely repeating. Trade relations are rarely (if ever) considered to be terminal. Any model of trade relations should take this into account. Conybeare does discuss the implications of repeating his games, but he provides no formal analysis. We formalize his argument here.

Central to any discussion of infinitely repeated games is the Folk Theorem (Rasmusen 1989, 92).[9] In an infinitely repeated N-person game with finite action sets at each repetition, any combination of actions observed in any finite number of repetitions is the unique outcome of some subgame perfect equilibrium given

Condition 1: The rate of time preference is zero, or positive and sufficiently small.

Condition 2: The probability that the game ends at any repetition is zero, or positive and sufficiently small.

Condition 3: The set of payoff combinations that strictly *Pareto-dominate* the minimax payoff combinations[10] in the mixed extension of the one-shot game is n-dimensional.[11]

---

9. The reference to the Folk Theorem is analogous to a traditional folk song; we ascribe its origins to no single author. The result of the Folk Theorem was widely known among game theorists as far back as the 1950s, despite the fact that no one had published it. Friedman (1971) deserves specific mention, however. His refinement of the Folk Theorem involving subgame perfect equilibria is noteworthy. Actually, ours is one of many versions of the folk theorem. See chapter 2 for a more intuitive version.

10. The strategy s^*_i is a set of $(n-1)$ minimax strategies chosen by all the players except i to keep $i's$ payoff as low as possible, regardless of how he responds (Rassmusen 1989, 104). Pareto domination implies that a set of payoff combinations provides greater utility to at least one player and gives no player lower utility than any other payoff combination.

11. The latter condition is one that applies to games in which there are three or more players. At this point in the chapter we are only dealing with two-player games. We deal with the ramifications of this third condition later, in discussing N-player games. See Rasmussen 1989 (92–93, 103–4), Aumann 1981 (12–13), and Fudenberg and Maskin 1986 for a discussion of the Folk Theorem.

In order to understand the implications of this theorem as applied to infinitely repeated games, we need to break it down into its constituent parts.

First, Condition 1 concerns the type of discount parameter being used. If the rate of time preference is zero, this means that the individual considers payoffs gained in one period of the game to be equal to the same payoffs gained in another period. In other words, the player does not value the present over the future. This rate is restricted to being zero or positive and sufficiently small to rule out two situations. The first is a perverse case in which individuals prefer future outcomes over past outcomes—in other words, their rate of time preference is negative. The second is a case in which an individual's time preference is very large. In this situation, future plays of the game may have no impact on individuals' current actions because they value the future so very little. Thus, the Folk Theorem holds when the future matters to the player in a nonperverse manner. The essential characteristic of this condition is that future play of the game is important to the players. If players do not value the payoffs from future games, they will play each stage of an infinitely repeated game as if it were a single-shot game.

Second, Condition 2 considers the probability of the game continuing. If a player knows that this is the last period of the game, then she may choose a different strategy since she realizes that she will not be receiving any further payoffs from this interaction. Regardless of her rate of time preference and her beliefs about how her action might affect the future actions of others, the individual will choose her best strategy with the constituent game. Thus, the Folk Theorem holds when players believe that their interaction will continue. The essential characteristic of this condition is that players do not know when the final game comes and cannot see it approaching. If there is a perceived end to the game, the Folk Theorem does not apply, and the characteristics of finitely repeated games hold.

The Folk Theorem posits that if a game is infinitely repeated many combinations of strategies are in equilibrium. Given that players value the payoffs of future games and believe that the game is ongoing, many sets of choices made by a player will be in equilibrium. This indeterminacy needs to be stressed. A large number of political scientists have argued that by infinitely repeating a game the new equilibrium is mutual cooperation. While mutual cooperation is one possible equilibrium, it is only one of many possible equilibria. Specfically, the Nash equilibria of the constituent game are always equilibria of the infinitely repeated game. Hence, mutual defection in the Prisoners' Dilemma game is still an equilibrium when infinitely repeated.

How does the Folk Theorem affect Conybeare's three trade games? We turn first to the Prisoners' Dilemma game. Shubik (1970), Taylor (1976, 1987), and Axelrod (1980a, 1980b, 1981, 1984) have introduced political scientists to the infinitely iterated Prisoners' Dilemma. Conybeare draws on Axelrod in particular. In Axelrod's formulation of the infinitely repeated Prisoners' Dilemma, cooperation may or may not emerge, depending on the importance each player places on future payoffs or, in other words, the manner in which the players discount the utility of the outcomes of future actions. Since mutual cooperation provides both players with higher payoffs than does mutual defection, we can expect to see players choose cooperation over defection if the conditions of the Folk Theorem hold. Mutual cooperation, however, is not the only equilibrium strategy. Ongoing trade relations between large countries *could* lead to mutual cooperation.

The indeterminant results of the Folk Theorem also apply to an infinitely iterated Hybrid Chicken–Stag Hunt game. While mutual cooperation is the equilibrium of the single-shot game, if the Folk Theorem holds, other combinations of strategies are also in equilibrium. Nevertheless, we can expect players to continue to choose mutual cooperation since it is *pareto efficient* to alternatives. Ongoing trade relations between small countries most likely will continue to remain cooperative.

How does the Folk Theorem affect the Asymmetric Trade game? While there is an indeterminacy to results of this game when infinitely repeated, as long as the large country possesses complete information a small country cannot credibly deter the large country from exploiting its situation. Without the ability to credibly deter a large country, the best the small country can do is continue unilaterally to cooperate; the outcome is no different than if the game were played once.

Games of Sequential Choice

Up to this point we have only used 2×2 matrix games involving simultaneous choice (complete and imperfect information) between two countries. There are, however, some problems with modeling trade conflict using simple matrix form games. The most obvious is that this approach neglects the fact that nations involved in trade disputes do not necessarily act simultaneously, without knowing the history of play between the two countries. In most cases, one nation moves first and another reacts to this initial action, knowing full well what the other has done. However, these simple matrix games, whether Prisoners' Dilemma, Chicken, Stag Hunt, Hybrid Chicken–Stag Hunt, or Asymmetric Trade, do not take sequence into account. In fact, the matrix presentation of this game disregards all information concerning the sequence of moves and the information revealed as players move. For example, if country X implements an import tariff on a specific good exported by country Y, country Y reacts knowing what action country X has taken. The choices made by these two players are sequential. This sequence is not modeled in this representation of the game. Thus, the rules of the game become obscured. In this form of the trade game:

> Strategies are now regarded not as complex sets of instructions but as abstract objects to be manipulated formally, without regard for their meaning. The outcomes or payoffs can now be given in tabular form or in mathematical formulas that may not reveal anything about the original extensive-form rules. It can be an interesting puzzle in cryptographic detection to try to infer the most likely information conditions, number of moves, and other elements of a game that is given in its strategic (matrix) form. (Shubik 1982, 67)

Simple matrix games do, however, offer some advantages. The most important of these is that they provide simple metaphors or analogies for us to use to describe political interactions. The Prisoners' Dilemma, Chicken, and Stag Hunt games have been used by many scholars in a productive manner in order to understand various political situations. While these games may not perfectly describe a situation, they do provide a first step in understanding social interactions. Conybeare's work fits this description. He offers an insightful view of the strategic aspects of international trade conflict and cooperation.

On the other hand, if we can explicitly model a situation more realistically there may be good reason to do so. Of course, any model involves simplification and parsimony, which should be a goal for any modeler. Nevertheless, Conybeare himself points to the need to consider the sequence of events. In the remainder of this section we present Conybeare's models in forms that take into account the sequential aspects of decision making in games with imperfect information.

An alternative form of modeling is through sequential choice or

Stackelberg games. These games are characterized by complete and perfect information, where all the players know the history of the game and all relevant payoffs. The basic form of a dynamic game with complete and perfect information takes the following form.

1. Player X chooses an action a_X from the feasible set A_X.
2. Player Y observes a_X and then selects an action a_Y from the feasible set A_Y.
3. Payoffs are $u_X(a_X, a_Y)$ and $u_Y(a_X, a_Y)$.

Such games possess three important characteristics: players' moves take place in sequence, all previous moves are observed before the next move is chosen, and players possess common knowledge about the payoffs. Such games are easily portrayed in the extensive form as a game tree (see figure 8). This approach is very flexible in that it can be used to model sequential decisions as well as problems of incomplete and imperfect information. The sequence of play is explicitly portrayed and can easily be seen in this form of game. The extensive form is also quite versatile. It can be used to model decisions in environments of perfect and complete information or under imperfect or incomplete information. In this section, we examine the extensive form, or dynamic games, under conditions of complete and perfect information and compare them to games of complete and imperfect information.

Conybeare points to the need to take such dynamics of choice into account: "Trade games cannot be treated as if they were static, with all the moves occurring in real time (i.e., all at once). A general theory of bilateral trade wars must presume that trade games are invariably iterated, in the sense that moves occur sequentially and players may have an opportunity to communicate, observe each others' behavior, change their own behavior, and possibly contrive enforceable agreements" (38). The problem is that these possibilities are not explicitly modeled by Conybeare. Dynamic sequential choice games provide the means for modeling sequential as well as repeated games.

How does sequential choice affect Conybeare's three models of trade conflict? To more completely answer this question we introduce the concepts of backwards induction and subgame perfect equilibrium. The notion of subgame perfectness is an equilibrium concept that is intrinsically linked to the extensive form game. We introduce this concept by examining a Prisoners' Dilemma game involving sequential choice. This game is characterized by complete and perfect

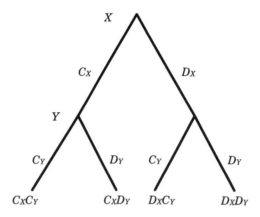

Fig. 8. The general extensive form of the two-player, single-play game

information (models of incomplete information are presented in chapter 5). Turn to figure 9; this figure depicts country X moving first, deciding whether to cooperate or defect. Country Y reacts to X's choice, also choosing between cooperation and defection. We can solve this game by following a procedure referred to as backwards induction. Look at the payoffs at the end of each branch of the game tree. Now compare those payoffs associated with branches that are connected by the most recent decision node. In this case we compare the $C_X C_Y$ branch with the $C_X D_Y$ branch payoffs and the $D_X C_Y$ branch with the $D_X D_Y$ branch. For each comparison, select the branch that produces the highest payoff for the player making the decision at the nearest node; in the case of the Prisoners' Dilemma this is $C_X D_Y$, associated with a payoff of 4 for Y, and $D_X D_Y$, which gives Y a payoff of 2. Next we move up to X's decision node. With complete and perfect information, X knows that Y will make choices that lead to the highest payoffs. Given this knowledge, X compares the payoffs associated with cooperation and defection, which are respectively determined by Y's decision to defect at each of these decision nodes. Faced with this choice, X chooses defect over cooperation.

Stackelberg equilibrium refers to the leader-follower aspects of sequential (perfect information) rather than simultaneous-move (imperfect information) games. As discussed above, sequentially played games sometimes have multiple Nash equilibria; often only one of these Nash equilibria can be determined through backwards induction. Stackelberg equilibrium implies sequential moves as well as a refinement of the Nash equilibrium concept. Stackelberg equilibria are a conceptual subset of the more general equilibrium concept of sub-

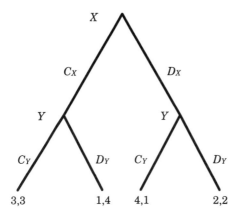

Fig. 9. Extensive form representation of Prisoners' Dilemma

game perfect equilibrium.[12] Mutual defection is the subgame perfect equilibrium for the sequential choice Prisoners' Dilemma game. This game possesses three subgames: (1) the entire game, starting from the node where X makes its decisions and all subsequent choices made by Y; (2) the subgame starting at Y's decision node following X's cooperation path; and (3) the subgame starting at Y's decision node following X's defection path. Subgame perfect equilibria take the history of a game into account by tracing the paths of the game tree through backwards induction; the basic rule is that all subgame perfect equilibria lie along the equilibrium path so that all equilibria make sense.

It should be pointed out that all the information contained in an extensive form game can be portrayed in matrix form; it is simply awkward for analysis. The reader should not conclude that matrix form games are only applicable to simultaneous choice games or that those only involving imperfect information and extensive form games are best for dynamic games with perfect information (see matrix 19). This matrix represents the extensive form game of figure 9 in matrix form. In a game such as that portrayed in figure 9 we can see that player Y has four strategies but two actions, since there are four contingencies. After observing player X's move, player Y chooses between two actions after player X has made a choice between two actions. These four strategies can be represented as C_yC_y, C_yD_y, D_yC_y, and D_yD_y. C_yC_y represents player Y's decision to cooperate if player X has chosen to cooperate and to cooperate if player X has chosen to defect. C_yD_y represents player Y's decision to cooperate if player X cooperates and to defect if player X defects. D_yC_y occurs

---

12. See chapter 2 for a discussion of subgame perfect equilibria.

Y

	C_YC_Y	C_YD_Y	D_YC_Y	D_YD_Y
C_X	3,3	3,3	1,4	1,4
D_X	4,1	2,2	4,1	2,2

X (label to left of rows)

Matrix 19. Matrix form of two-player, sequential move Prisoners' Dilemma

when player Y defects if player X cooperates and cooperates if player X defects. D_yD_y, on the other hand, represents player Y's decision to defect if player X has chosen to cooperate and to defect if player X defects. Player X has only two strategies and two actions, since there is only one contingency for player X, the opening move. The payoffs are derived from figure 9, matching player Y's strategy to the contingency based on player X's choice. Hence, the combination of strategies, (cooperate, C_yC_y) is associated with a payoff of (3,3) while (defect, C_yC_y) is associated with a payoff of (4,1). With the C_yC_y strategy, player Y cooperates whether player X chooses to cooperate or defect. While we can represent a sequentially played game in matrix form it is awkward to analyze. The extensive form will be used from now on to portray games of imperfect and complete information as well as games of incomplete information (to be presented in chapter 5).

For all three games, Prisoners' Dilemma, Hybrid Chicken–Stag Hunt (fig. 10), and Asymmetric Trade (fig. 11), sequential choice and simultaneous outcomes are the same. All three of Conybeare's hypotheses remain unaffected in this game environment. Nevertheless, we want to emphasize that we get the same results relying exclusively on game theory. We do not need to rely on ad hoc non–game theoretic explanations. These results, moreover, have special relevance to the Asymmetric Trade game. Do sequential choices make it more tempting for a small country to attempt to deter a large country from defecting? Not as long as there is a likely end to the game. As long as there is a final decision node, large countries will always defect. Given this information, a small country will only punish itself by choosing to cooperate at the first node of the game. Assuming that it seeks to maximize its payoff, a small country in an Asymmetric Trade game will cooperate even when moving first in a sequential choice game to avoid what it regards as the disastrous outcome of mutual defection.

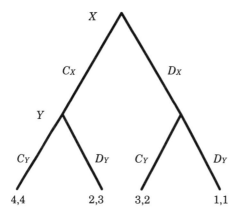

Fig. 10. Extensive form representation of Hybrid Chicken–Stag Hunt

When does sequential choice make a difference? It makes a difference when a simultaneous choice or (imperfect information) game possesses a mixed strategy equilibrium. Such a game is Chicken. In such a game under simultaneous choice conditions, players mix their choices across cooperation and defection according to expected payoff calculations. In the sequential form, no mixing takes place (see fig. 12). The player who chooses first is allowed to dictate the options to the player choosing later. In this case the first player can defect first, forcing the second player to unilaterally cooperate. Given complete and perfect information, the first player knows that the second player will choose cooperation to avoid the disaster of mutual defection. Sequential choice guarantees that mutual defection is avoided, but it also puts the player choosing second always in an unfavorable position. Sequential decisions only make a difference when there is no pure strategy equilibrium or more than one pure strategy equilibrium.[13]

Just as we demonstrated above how a sequential game can be portrayed in matrix form, a simultaneous choice game (or, more precisely, a game of imperfect information) can be represented in the extensive form. Figure 13 is an extensive form game of Chicken with imperfect information. The dashed line connecting the two-player Y decision nodes represents the information set containing both contingencies involving player X's choices.

While Conybeare's hypotheses are not affected by making these games sequential with perfect and complete information, as opposed

---

13. This also assumes finite plays.

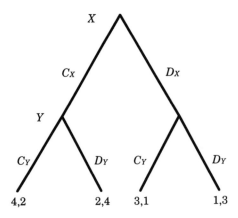

Fig. 11. Extensive form representation of Asymmetric Trade

to simultaneous choice involving imperfect and complete information, these can be extremely important distinctions for many games. Our modeling approach more precisely follows Conybeare's own discussion. In this manner, we take advantage of the strengths of game theory. We have provided an alternative approach to modeling these games relying exclusively on game theory.

N-Player Games of Trade

So far we have only dealt with games involving two players. Yet many strategic situations arise in which more than two players are involved. Due to the nature of international economic relations, many players are often involved. Multilateral agreements play a particularly promi-

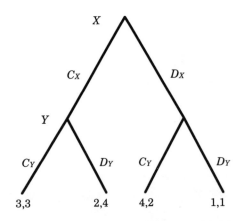

Fig. 12. Extensive form representation of Chicken

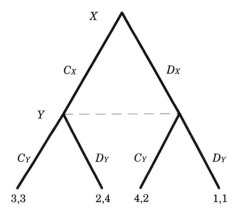

Fig. 13. Extensive form representation of Chicken with imperfect information

nent role in international trade. What happens when additional people are added to the strategic interaction? Do additional players make a difference? Yes, additional players do make a difference. John von Neumann and Oskar Morgenstern (1944) note how additional players can substantially affect a game. Include an infinite number of players and a noncooperative game resembles N-player maximization problems solved simultaneously. Each player treats all other players as part of the broader environment. In microeconomics we see such behavior in perfectly competitive markets. Many-player games are characterized by limiting properties, wherein every player calculates his or her expected utility in the manner described in chapter 3 regarding decision theory. Multilateral trade relations, however, cannot always be characterized as many-player games (or indeterminantly large N-player games). Such multilateral arrangements involve a small number of (but more than two) players. Such games characterize oligopolistic markets, political coalitions, cartels, and multilateral negotiations and agreements. In this section we focus on this variety of N-player games (small-number as opposed to many player games). All involve three or more players.

Conybeare devotes considerable attention to "large-number trade wars." He emphasizes that free trade cannot be characterized as a public good. Conybeare persuasively argues that free trade is excludable and rival and further asserts that his basic game structures stand. Conybeare, however, offers no formal model of N-player games. In this section of this chapter, we formally present some N-player games and provide a theoretical base to support Conybeare's hypotheses in an N-player environment (for which he provides no formal analysis).

We focus our attention on N-player games involving few but more than two players. We do not restrict our examination to the limiting conditions of large N-player games. We demonstrate here what happens when a few additional players are added.

What happens to Conybeare's games when they are transformed from two-player games to N-player games? In the case of the Prisoners' Dilemma, Hybrid Chicken–Stag Hunt, and Asymmetric Trade games there is no difference in equilibria in either the two-player or the N-player form. In fact, if all strategy sets in a game are eliminated by domination except for the set of strategies $(s_1, \ldots, s_{i-1}, s_i^*, s_{i+1}, \ldots, s_n)$, then these strategies constitute the Nash equilibria for the N-player game. Therefore, N-player Prisoners' Dilemma and Hybrid Chicken–Stag Hunt games are characterized by universal defection and universal cooperation as their respective Nash equilibria. As for the N-player Asymmetric Trade game, in which there is one large country and $N - 1$ small countries, the big country possesses a dominant strategy to defect while all small powers have a dominant strategy to continue to cooperate. Given these dominant strategies, the Nash equilibrium for the N-player Asymmetric Trade game is for the large power to defect and for all $N - 1$ small countries to cooperate. This situation is described by Conybeare as hegemonic predation.

We focus our attention here on solving collective action problems. In the remainder of this section, we present a trade game involving a three-player Prisoners' Dilemma game. We also develop an N-player game with leadership. Our analysis is drawn from Bianco and Bates (1990), Quiñones (1992), and Quiñones and Gates (1993). We begin by looking at three players facing the same payoffs as those presented in figure 9. What difference does a third player make? Consider this third player, Z, who makes a decision with complete and perfect information following players X and Y. Analyzing this game as before, the equilibrium is $\{D,D,D\}$, which is analogous to the $\{D,D\}$ equilibrium of the two-player Prisoners' Dilemma game. In fact, the likelihood of mutual cooperation in the three-player game is less likely than in the two-player environment.

Consider the three-player game as a game in which the players have the option of forming coalitions. In the case of the three-player game each has the option of forming a coalition of three, two, or one. A coalition of three cooperators receives a higher payoff than a coalition of three defectors, but one defector gets a higher payoff than any coalition of two or three regardless of whether they all cooperate or defect. Moreover, a coalition of two defectors obtains higher payoffs than does a coalition of two cooperators. These factors make the incentive to defect even stronger than in the two player game.[14]

This same payoff ordering holds in the N-player environment. The distinguishing characteristics of the N-player and two-player versions of the Prisoners' Dilemma game is that: *(a)* all players have the dominant strategy to defect, *(b)* if every player follows his or her dominant strategy, all players end up with a Pareto inferior outcome with mutual cooperation, and *(c)* given nonbinding commitments, there is always an incentive for a player to defect.

We now turn to a similar game involving N-players comprising a trade regime. The regime is a long-term trade agreement among a set of member nation-states. We therefore assume that players will interact in the future. The game is thus characterized by infinite repetition and discounting. Nation-states interact over a series of rounds in a game, where each iteration is designated as t. Each player makes its decision with imperfect information, not knowing what other nation-states have decided. The strategy set for each follower contains two choices:

$$s_t = 0, \quad \text{defect}$$
$$s_t = 1, \quad \text{cooperate.}$$

All countries are rewarded with an evenly distributed proportion of total benefits, B_n. Total benefits, $B(s_t)$, are derived from the strategies, $S(s_{i_t})$, of all nation-states. The resulting vector of all of these stratgies is represented in the equation

$$B(s_t) = a_1[s_{1_t} + s_{2_t} + \ldots + s_{N_t}].$$

Payoffs for each player's strategy at iteration (t) involve dividing the goods created by the regime among all N members. The payoffs for cooperation and defection can be expressed as

$$V_{Ni_t}(S_{Ni_t}) = \frac{B(S_t)}{N} - c \quad \text{if cooperate}$$

$$V_{Ni_t}(S_{Ni_t}) = \frac{B(S_t)}{N} \quad \text{if defect.}$$

Each player possesses a dominant strategy to defect at each iteration of the game. This is because cooperation always involves a cost, c, while defection results in no cost. Given the nature of individual

---

14. The good here is a public good for which excludability is the primary problem.

benefits, $B(s_{i_t})$, defecting is the dominant strategy no matter how many players cooperate or defect. Nevertheless, universal cooperation always provides a higher payoff for all actors than does universal defection. Regardless of the number of countries that can benefit from mutual cooperation, an individual nation-state always has an incentive to defect since the benefits from defecting always exceed the gains from cooperation. In this respect, N-player Prisoners' Dilemma is no different from the two-player version of the game. As the number of cooperators or defectors increases, the payoff to a single nation i follows either a payoff vector from cooperating or from defecting. Look to table 1 for further illustration of this point. This table presents the payoffs for a country in a 10-nation trade regime. From this table it is evident that defection always provides a higher payoff even when one or more other players are defecting.

Players make maximizing decisions based on the actions of other players. Several parameters shape the payoffs associated with different strategies. Since every nation-state has an incentive to defect from the economic regime, this model possesses characteristics of a collective action problem. In this way the regime produces public goods that are nonexcludable and nonrival. Note, however, that these nation-states can expect to interact with each other in the future. As such this is a game of repeated play. The Folk Theorem (as noted earlier) demonstrates that, if discount rates are high enough, full cooperation can be maintained as a subgame perfect equilibrium.[15] In such repeated games, players often rely on a trigger strategy. A trigger strategy is a strategy in which players follow a particular action until the behavior of another player (or players) serves to "trigger" a change in action. For example, a nation-state will cooperate in the regime until someone else defects, in which case punishment is triggered. Such a trigger strategy can be characterized as possessing two phases, a cooperative phase and a trigger phase.[16] As long as the Folk Theorem applies to this game, there exists an equilibrium whereby one nation-state will be willing to punish another for the sake of higher future payoffs, even in the face of short-term losses due to the costs of punishing. This makes intuitive sense, if one compares the payoffs over an infinite time horizon to some short-term period, so that

15. In this case the payoff from defecting is valued more, while future gains from cooperation are valued less. Given a discount rate that is sufficiently high, a game most likely will be one shot. Therefore, any game that depends on a large number of repetitions also relies on the discount rate not being too high.

16. See Fudenberg and Tirole 1991 (185–86). Also see Green and Porter 1984 on trigger-price strategies and Friedman 1971 for the original work on trigger strategies.

TABLE 1. Payoffs to Player 1 When $a_1 = 2$ and $c = 1$ in a 10 Player Trade Game

s_t of N_1	$S_{s_t}=9$	$S_{s_t}=8$	$S_{s_t}=7$	$S_{s_t}=6$	$S_{s_t}=5$	$S_{s_t}=4$	$S_{s_t}=3$	$S_{s_t}=2$	$S_{s_t}=1$	$S_{s_t}=0$
Number of Member Nation-States That Select the Strategy $s_t = 1$ (cooperate)										
$s_{1_t}=1$ (cooperate)	1	.8	.6	.4	.2	0	−.2	−.4	−.6	−.8
$s_{1_t}=0$ (defect)	1.8	1.6	1.4	1.2	1.0	.8	.6	.4	.2	0

players are willing to carry out punishment to encourage cooperation. The Folk Theorem tells us that cooperation is possible if an N-player game is infinitely repeated, but it does not necessitate universal cooperation. Universal defection is still an equilibrium result. These results formally support what Conybeare contends with words about N-player trade games.

Leadership

One situation left unexplored by many analysts of international trade is the role of leadership in securing cooperation, that is, global free trade. In the remainder of this section we draw from Quiñones and Gates (1993) for a model of regime leadership. Alt, Calvert, and Humes (1988) is one of the few formal models to show how cooperation can be obtained over time in a regime with the existence of a hegemon. A hegemon here implies a country significantly larger in economic size than other countries. With this size comes the ability to serve as a regime leader. In the game presented in this section, we characterize the hegemon as a leader to distinguish it from Conybeare's predatory hegemon. Although Alt, Calvert, and Humes suggest that in some instances cooperation does not necessitate the existence of a hegemon, if defection is imminent, the hegemon's presence can induce cooperation. They argue that strategic reputation building by the hegemon is the key to maintaining cooperation in an iterated game. Although Alt, Calvert, and Humes's model is one of the first (and few) attempts at illustrating formally how cooperation can be maintained in a regime, the authors do not address how actors within the regime affect one another. The model presented here extends some of the concepts examined by Alt, Calvert, and Humes by not only generalizing the static concept of a hegemon into a dynamic leadership role but by including multiple actors. The inclusion of multiple actors permits us to illustrate how countries affect one another and how leaders (hegemons) influence these interactions. Moreover, we can model such multilateral trade relationships within a game theoretic framework.

To understand the nature and role of leadership in international economic regimes we include leaders in our analysis. Leaders serve the role of distributing residuals produced by the regime to followers, and in so doing they both reward and punish. As a residual claimant, leaders receive a share equal to s $(0 < s < 1)$, which is a portion of each benefit plus all undistributed remaining benefits. Now a comment is in order. Conybeare directly criticizes another production by teams model applied to international trade (e.g., Yarbrough and Yarbrough 1985, 1986). He makes two arguments: *(a)* the gains from trade are not controlled by the hegemon, and *(b)* hegemons have no incentive to be leaders of free trade systems when they can enforce bilateral trade contracts themselves. Before proceeding, these criticisms need to be addressed. As for how a hegemon controls the residuals from trade, we argue that the gains from trade also stem from the international rules of trade. The hegemon in many ways is able to dictate these rules and use them to reward and punish other members of the system. As for whether hegemons will be strictly predatory or benevolent, we contend that they function as maximizing agents; if serving as a regime leader, provides a higher long-term payoff than predatory bilateral actions do, then a large country will engage in such activity. Regime leaders may obtain significant payoffs by shaping and determining the rules of international trade to their own advantage. So the issue boils down to what activity produces larger long-term payoffs, bilateral predation or international leadership. We assume the latter; Conybeare assumes the former.

This is a point to note. We are able to clearly distinguish our work from Conybeare's here in that we rely on different assumptions about the relative payoffs of bilateral predation and international leadership. In operationalizing the payoffs associated with different outcomes, we posit a very different game structure than Conybeare does. In this way the role of clear assumptions is evident.

Let us now return to our N-person trade leadership game. Recall that each of the regular nation-states makes its initial decision with imperfect information, not knowing what other nation-states have decided. Leaders, on the other hand, move afterward with complete and perfect information. We now examine the payoffs obtained by a leader of such an international regime. A leader's payoffs come from some portion of the total benefits produced by the trade regime. The portion of the total benefits available to the leader depends on the number punished for defecting. Punishment of the followers means that the leader withholds rewards from defectors. The payoff function for a leader is characterized as

$$V_{i_t} = \sigma b(s_t) + \frac{x}{N(1 - \sigma)b(s_t)}$$

where $\sigma b(s_t)$ is the portion of benefits, x is the number of players sanctioned for defection, and N is the total number of regime members.[17] A leader's payoff is affected by the actions taken by other members of the regime. As the proportion of defectors rises, the payoff to the leader grows. In this way, the leader has a stake in the total benefits created by the regime plus the special role as leader, sanctioning members that do not cooperate.

Payoffs for followers (other members of the trade regime) are influenced by the stream of benefits produced by the regime as well as the costs associated with cooperating. Both of these parameters are seen in the payoff function for followers at any t iteration of the game. The behavior of other players affects the stream of benefits produced by the regime, but unlike the leader they do not exercise sanctions against defecting states. These payoffs are presented as

$$V_{i_t}(s_t) = \frac{(1 - \sigma)b(s_t)}{N} - c \quad A1 \text{ cooperate} \cap \text{ get reward}$$

$$V_{i_t}(s_t) = \frac{(1 - \sigma)b(s_t)}{N} \quad A2 \text{ defect} \cap \text{ get reward}$$

$$V_{i_t}(s_t) = 0 \quad A3 \text{ defect} \cap \text{ get punished}.$$

Given these payoff functions, followers utilize two different trigger strategies. The first, the grim trigger (g-trigger), means that a follower cooperates until another follower defects or a leader fails to reward after cooperation, such that

g-trigger $t = 0$:   cooperate
  $t > 0$:   cooperate if $b(s_t^*) = b_N$ and all followers, f, are rewarded, i, for all $t^* < t$, defect otherwise.

---

17. This payoff is a generalization of the payoff to Bianco and Bates's enhanced leader (1990).

Alternatively, followers will utilize a strategic trigger wherein they defect when it is in their best interest for that iteration of the game, such that

s-trigger $t = 0$: cooperate

$t > 0$: cooperate if $b(s_t^*) \geq B_{n-1}$ and the leader rewards follower, i, on all $t^* < t$, defect otherwise.

With the s-trigger strategy, followers will cooperate as long as the benefits of cooperating exceed the benefits of defecting. Given these strategies, cooperation can occur without a leader.[18] Such cooperation, however, is difficult to sustain. There is always an incentive to defect. Such a defection, in turn, can set off other players' triggers, resulting in widespread defection.

A leader can play a critical role in sustaining cooperation. Threats of fellow followers can sustain cooperation (that is, the grim trigger strategy), but the rewards and punishments of leaders do play a role. Leaders of regimes observe each follower's strategy choice, s_{i_t}, for each iteration, t, of the game, rewarding and punishing each follower separately. In this manner, the leader establishes an incentive system to influence the actions of members of a regime. A leader serves the role of distributing the residuals produced by the trade regime and sanctioning all defecting followers. Leaders follow an L-trigger strategy whereby they create an incentive system by rewarding and punishing followers:

L-trigger $t = 0$: reward all followers, i

$t > 0$: reward follower i if $s_{Ni_t}^* = 1$ on all $t^* < t$, punish nation-state N_i otherwise.

Under such conditions, with such leadership capabilities, cooperation can be enforced through punishment. Leadership in the form of a hegemon can play a more significant role in attaining cooperation than simply repeating the N-player game. Our model of leadership follows from a broader set of models known as principal-agent analysis. More directly our model reflects the work of Holmström's pro-

---

18. These two follower triggers reflect the b-trigger and s-trigger strategies in Bianco and Bates 1990.

duction by teams model (1982) and, in turn, Bianco and Bates's leadership game (1990) as well as Miller (1992), which can be characterized as iterated production by teams games. The game presented here is a further generalization of the Bianco and Bates game.

Such a game serves as an alternative model and conception to Conybeare's predatory hegemon. We do see leadership and multilateral cooperation in international trade. Trade can be characterized as an iterated game where the game is unlikely to end and international actors have consistent expectations about other players' intentions to reciprocate. As long as these two conditions persist (a low probability of the game ending and mutual expectations about reciprocity), we can expect to see cooperation. If these conditions are called into question, leaders can serve to facilitate cooperation by enforcing compliance.

Conclusion

Trade games can be used to model the politics and institutions that affect strategic trade interactions and reciprocity. Conybeare's analytical structure, which focuses on country size, leads to a series of interesting conclusions regarding two large countries, two small countries, and asymmetric trade conflict. In their simple 2×2, single-shot format, we would expect to see (as does Conybeare) mutual defection, mutual defection, and unilateral cooperation across these three games. These outcomes hold for sequential choice and finitely repeated games as well. The game played between two large countries (Prisoners' Dilemma) can change if the game is infinitely repeated and the Folk Theorem applies. N-player games can also be used to explicitly model multilateral interactions and collective action problems. Results for N-player games do not change unless an explicit third party, a leader, is incorporated into the game. For all of Conybeare's games, because each equilibrium is influenced by the principle of domination, the results are robust.

What we have attempted to demonstrate in this chapter is how different circumstances can be explicitly modeled within games. This demonstrates the relevance and importance of clearly specifying the structure of the game. We also demonstrate the need to justify modeling choices. By explicitly modeling the structure of a game we exploit one of the strengths of this methodology. By clearly specifying one's modeling choices and the structure of a game we are able to avoid relying on non–game theoretic factors to justify our conclusions. In this chapter we have shown how games can be modeled with simul-taneous and sequential play, with single play and repeated play (with either finite or infinite time horizons), and with either two players or N players. In the next chapter we examine games under conditions of incomplete information.

CHAPTER 5

Information and Transitions to Democracy: An Examination of Przeworski's *Democracy and the Market*

Information plays a critical role in many political interactions. When political actors must make choices under uncertainty, they may act differently than they would if they possessed complete and perfect information. This chapter stresses how uncertainty can make a difference. More specifically, we compare games of complete and incomplete information.[1] We will also discuss games of imperfect information.

To more clearly explicate our discussion of incomplete information games, we examine several models of policy reform. We focus particular attention on the models developed by Adam Przeworski in *Democracy and the Market* (1991).[2] Przeworski's work is an insightful examination of the strategic interactions that characterize the politics of democratization and privatization. In this chapter, we first present Przeworski's model of political liberalization. After discussing how this model is underspecified, we then show how certain game theoretic concepts can be utilized to better specify this model of policy reform. We take Przeworski's games and extend them to both demonstrate the significance of information in such strategic interactions, and demonstrate how Przeworski's conclusions can be strengthened with our analysis.[3] The chapter proceeds as follows. We start with an examination of Przeworski's models of political liberalization. We then extend these models and discuss how the games are interrelated.

The theme of this chapter is information. In particular, we emphasize the difference between incomplete and complete information. Players playing games of complete information possess knowledge

---

1. Please refer to chapter 2 for a more detailed discussion of complete and incomplete information as well as perfect and imperfect information.

2. This is Adam Przeworski's *Democracy and the Market: Political and Economic Reform in Eastern Europe and Latin America* (1991).

3. Przeworski presents many models in this book. We attempt to address only one of them here.

about the structure of the game and associated payoffs. Players playing games of incomplete information do not know the payoffs associated with all choices. Games of incomplete information allow us to analyze strategic interactions that involve uncertainty on the part of one or both players.[4] Harsanyi (1967) introduced a way to model games of incomplete information by introducing the concept of Nature. Nature moves in such a way that payoffs are determined for the players of the game. Players must make their choices without knowing what move Nature has made. With incomplete information about payoffs, players may make different decisions than they would make with complete information. In this manner, incomplete information can make a difference.

Models of Democratic Transition

Przeworski's Models of Political Liberalization

We start our analysis by focusing on a set of models developed by Przeworski. Next we present two alternative models of political liberalization. Then we analyze a repeated game of reputation building. Przeworski's models examine the strategic interaction between liberalizers within an authoritarian government and mobilizers within civil society. Przeworski refers to this as the period of liberalization. He presents several alternatives that stem from liberalization, "either to incorporate the few groups that can be incorporated and to repress everyone else, returning to the authoritarian stasis, or to open the political agenda to the problem of institutions, that is, of democracy" (60). Refer to figure 14 for the extensive form representation of this interaction.[5] The liberalizers make the initial move, deciding between opening up the political process (open) and maintaining the status quo (stay tough). If a decision to stay tough is made, the outcome is a strong dictatorship (SDIC). If a decision to open up the political process is made, civil society is given an opportunity to choose between entering into a compact (enter) with the state or organizing politically (organize). If civil society enters, the outcome is broad dictatorship (BDIC). Given a decision to politically organize, the liberalizers must decide whether to further political reforms (turn into reformers) or to repress the organized political activity. If the liber-

---

4. By uncertainty we mean that players have incomplete information and are thus uncertain about the payoffs.

5. Refer to Przeworski 1991 (54–66) for a discussion of this process and this game. The game tree appears on page 62.

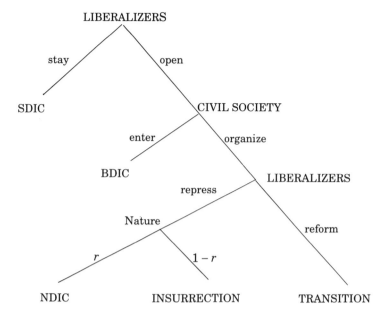

Fig. 14. Przeworski's model of democratic transition. (From Przeworski 1991, 62. Reproduced by permission of Cambridge University Press.)

alizers allow further political reform, political transition to democracy (Transition) is the outcome. Repression can be successful, leading to a narrow dictatorship (NDIC) with a probability of r. On the other hand, repression could be unsuccessful (with a probability of $1 - r$) which leads to widespread insurrection (Insurrection). Keep in mind, Nature plays a role in this game. This is a game of incomplete information. We can summarize this game as follows.

1. Liberalizers (L) choose an action, a_L, from the feasible set, A_L, where $A_L = \{stay\ with\ hardliners,\ open\}$, and where *stay with hardliners* ends the game, providing the payoffs to both players associated with the outcome of SDIC.
2. Civil society (CS) observes the liberalizers' choice under perfect and complete information. If the liberalizers choose *open*, then civil society chooses an action, a_{CS}, from the feasible set $A_{CS} = \{enter,\ organize\}$, where *enter* ends the game with the payoffs to both players associated with the BDIC outcome.
3. Liberalizers observe civil society's move with complete and perfect information (as well as perfect recall of its own earlier move). If the preceding choices were *open* and *organize*, liberalizers choose either *repress* or *turn into reformers*, where *turn*

into reformers ends the game with the payoffs to both players associated with Transition.

4. If the preceding choices were *open, organize,* and *repress,* Nature determines the payoffs for both players associated with the outcomes NDIC and Insurrection, and the game ends.

Using this game structure, Przeworski alters the players' payoffs associated with these different outcomes to explore facets of political liberalization. In the remainder of this section we present each of Przeworski's variations of this game.

Figure 15 portrays the payoffs and structure of the game that would lead to no reform and the maintenance of a strong dictatorship (SDIC). The structure of the game is the same as that represented in figure 14. The payoff ordering for civil society for this situation and all variations of this game is Transition > BDIC > Insurrection > SDIC > NDIC. We have assigned payoffs to each of these outcomes such that Transition = 5, BDIC = 4, Insurrection = 3, SDIC = 2, and NDIC = 1. The payoff ordering for the liberalizers within the government in this situation is BDIC > SDIC > Transition > NDIC > Insurrection. We have assigned payoffs to each of these outcomes such that BDIC = 5, SDIC = 4, Transition = 3, NDIC = 2, and Insurrection = 1. To solve for equilibrium in this game we use backwards induction. Start with the final move by Nature with probabilities of r and $1 - r$. Nature's move determines whether repression leads to narrow dictatorship (NDIC), which sits at the end of one branch of the game tree, or insurrection, which sits at the end of the other branch of the tree.

In this case the two outcomes associated with repression are narrow dictatorship (NDIC) and Insurrection, which give payoffs of 2 and 1, respectively. The value of r shapes the expected payoff associated with a decision to repress any organized political activity. As the payoffs are set up here, liberalizers have a dominant strategy to choose reform over repression since a payoff of 3 is greater than either 1 or 2. (So, even with $r = 1$, where successful repression is guaranteed, reform will be selected over repression.) Following the game tree backward to the next decision node, civil society must decide whether to enter the government to form a broad dictatorship (BDIC) or organize politically. Given backwards induction, we compare the payoffs associated with BDIC (4) to Transition (5). Civil society chooses to organize. Now move backward one more step to the liberalizers' decision to open or stay tough. Staying tough results in the continuation of a strong dictatorship (a payoff ranking of 4). Compare this to

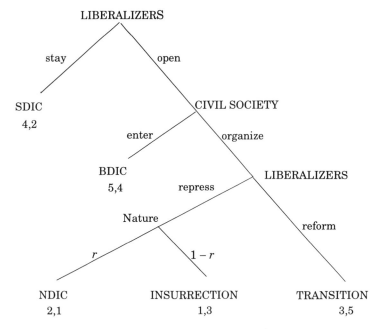

Fig. 15. First variation of Przeworski's model. (Data provided by the authors, adapted from Przeworski 1991, 62.)

opening up, which eventually leads to transition with a payoff of 3. Since the payoff associated with SDIC is greater than the payoff for Transition, liberalizers will stay tough and no reform takes place. The equilibrium for this game is thus {(*stay with hardliners, reform*), *organize*}. Note how we present this equilibrium: the liberalizers' decisions in equilbrium are grouped in parentheses. These choices reflect decisions that follow the path of backwards induction. So in this case *reform* is a choice that occurs at the final decision node of liberalizers even though this choice is actually precluded by the preceding decision to *stay with hardliners*. In this way, this format for expressing the equilibrium provides information about the path of backwards induction.

What payoffs are needed to attain Transition? See figure 16. Here the payoff ordering for the liberalizers is BDIC > Transition > SDIC > NDIC > Insurrection. Using backwards induction, we look first to the last decision node. Here Transition (with a payoff of 4) is strictly preferred to repression (with payoffs of 1 for Insurrection or 2 for NDIC). Again, civil society prefers Transition (5) to BDIC (4). But now liberalizers value Transition (4) more highly than the status quo, SDIC (3). In this case, liberalizers choose to open up the political

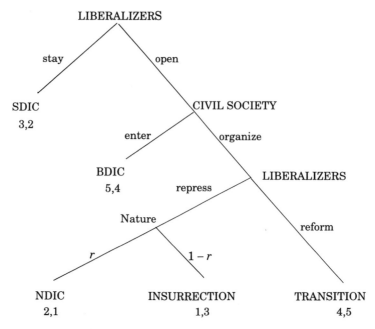

Fig. 16. Second variation of Przeworski's model. (Data provided by the authors, adapted from Przeworski 1991, 62.)

process which leads to transition to democracy. Hence, the equilibrium is {*(open, reform), organize*}. In this example, Przeworski has set up the game so that the payoffs directly determine the outcome. The game portrayed in figure 16 is not affected by the incomplete information associated with the success of repression. Payoffs associated with this game make this uncertainty irrelevant to the determination of equilibria. Information, nevertheless, can play a significant role in determining the equilibria of a game. Przeworski posits a game in which incomplete information plays a critical role in shaping an outcome that leads to the transition to democracy. Figure 17 represents this situation. Both players face incomplete information; neither player knows if repression will be successful or not. As with the game described in figure 15, nature dictates the success of repression with a probability of r, which leads to an outcome of narrow dictatorship (NDIC). Insurrection stems from unsuccessful repression; Nature determines this lack of success with a probability of $1 - r$. In this game, narrow dictatorship is preferred to Transition. The payoff ordering for the liberalizers in this situation is BDIC > SDIC > NDIC > Transition > Insurrection. The respective ordinal ranking of the payoffs associated with each of these outcomes is BDIC = 5, SDIC = 4,

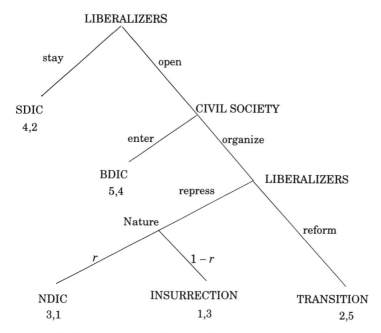

Fig. 17. Third variation of Przeworski's model. (Data provided by the authors, adapted from Przeworski 1991, 62.)

NDIC = 3, Transition = 2, and Insurrection = 1. Here, it is clear, the liberalizers have little interest in Transition.

To solve for the equilibria associated with this game we again use backwards induction. As before, begin the analysis by examining the final decision made by the liberalizers: whether or not to repress organized groups. Now two outcomes associated with repression (NDIC and Insurrection) produce payoffs of 3 and 1, respectively. With these payoffs the value of r makes a difference if the expected payoff associated with a decision to repress any organized political activity is greater than the payoff for Transition. The value of r represents the probability of successful repression. This probability is determined by Nature and is unknown to either player. The expected payoff for repression is determined in the same manner as is any decision theory calculation. In this case, we multiply the payoffs and their respective probabilities, such that

$$E_L(repression) = (r)3 + (1 - r)1. \tag{5.1}$$

Using the expected payoff for repression, we can determine the value of r needed to entice liberalizers to choose Transition over repression. To do this, set the expected payoff for repression equal to the expected payoff for Transition (which is 2, given complete information). With these payoffs, we see that if $r = 0.5$ liberalizers would be indifferent between repression and Transition. We find three equilibria structured by liberalizers' beliefs about r, including:

> *Case 1:* {*(stay, reform), organize*}. This occurs if $r < 0.5$, causing $E_L(reform) > E_L(repress)$.

If $r < 0.5$, liberalizers will choose reform over repression despite preferring narrow dictatorship over Transition; in this case, the danger of Insurrection is too great with such a low probability of successful repression. Civil society, looking ahead and reasoning backward, chooses to organize over enter. This in turn induces liberalizers to stay with the hardliners. This equilibrium leads to an outcome of SDIC.

> *Case 2:* {*(open, repress), enter*}. This equilbrium is evident when $r > 0.5$.

If both players know that $r > 0.5$, civil society also makes an expected utility calculation on the payoffs it will obtain if the liberalizers choose repression. Given such a value of r and using the logic of backwards induction, the expected payoff to civil society for organizing is less than 2.5. Comparing this payoff to the payoff 4 associated with BDIC, civil society will choose to enter rather than organize. Given that the liberalizers prefer BDIC to SDIC, BDIC is the outcome associated with this equilibrium strategy combination.

> *Case 3:* {*(open, ($\frac{1}{2}$ reform, $\frac{1}{2}$ repress)), ($\frac{2}{3}$ enter, $\frac{1}{3}$ organize)*}, when $r = 0.5$.

This is a mixed strategy equilibrium. When $r = 0.5$, liberalizers are indifferent between reform and repress. Using backwards induction, we can then compare the expected payoffs of civil society between organize and enter. By entering, civil society guarantees itself a payoff of 4, such that $E_{CS}(enter) = 4$. When civil society chooses to organize, the mixed strategy of the liberalizers must be taken into account, such that

$$E_{CS}(organize) = r(1 - p)1 + (1 - r)(1 - p)3 + (p)5.$$

Here, the payoff of 1 results when repression is successful (r); the payoff of 3 comes when repression is unsuccessful ($1 - r$); and the

payoff of 5 follows a decision by liberalizers to reform with a probability (p). Substituting in 0.5 for r we get

$$E_{CS}(organize) = 0.5(1 - p)1 + 0.5(1 - p)3 + (p)5.$$

By setting $E_{CS}(organize) = E_{CS}(repress)$ we can calculate p (liberalizers' mixed strategy for reform and repress).
   This simplifies to

$$4 = 2 + 3p,$$

and

$$p = 2/3.$$

Drawing from this calculation, it is evident that liberalizers choose to
reform two-thirds of the time.
   Now we move up the game tree to liberalizers' decision regarding
stay and *enter*. By setting $E_L(stay) = E_L(open)$, civil societies' mix
can be calculated. Such that

$$4 = g5 + (1 - g)[r(1 - p)3 + (1 - r)(1 - p)1 + p2].$$

This simplifies to

$$g = 2/3.$$

In words, civil society will use a mixed strategy in which they *enter*
two-thirds of the time. This combination of equilibrium strategies
leads to the mixed strategy equilibrium identified in *Case 3*.
   So how can this game get to a point of political transition? What
payoffs are needed to induce political actors to make the decisions that
lead to regime transformation? Przeworski describes a game like the
one portrayed in figure 17, but one in which the belief about r changes
after the game has begun (or at least after civil society begins to
organize politically). Przeworski presents this case intuitively, where
liberalizers' beliefs about r change after civil society begins to organize. In this situation, society believes that r is low, hence its decision
to organize. Observing this decision, the liberalizers' belief about r
falls to a point where the probability of successful repression is below
0.5. Przeworski does not provide a rigorous analysis of how players
make decisions under such uncertainty. In the remainder of this sec-

tion we show how Bayes' rule and perfect Bayesian equilibrium can be used to analyze such a game.

This discussion of how decisions are made under uncertainty can be more rigorously analyzed using Bayes' rule. This mechanism allows us to incorporate subjective probability or beliefs into our calculation of equilibria. Bayes' rule is:

$$p(A|B) = \frac{p(B|A)p(A)}{p(B|A)P(A) + p(B|\neg A)p(\neg A)}, \qquad (5.2)$$

where $p(A|B)$ is the conditional probability that an event, A, will take place given the occurrence of B; $p(B|A)$ is the conditional probability of B given A; $p(A)$ is the prior probability that A would occur; and $p(B|A)p(A) + (B|\neg A)p(\neg A)$ is the marginal likelihood of seeing A given either B or $\neg B$ (not B).[6] In the case of this political liberalization game, liberalizers update their beliefs when society begins to organize, calling into question the liberalizers' prior beliefs about the probability of successful repression (r). Society's action sends a signal to the liberalizers regarding r.

One way to determine an equilibrium when beliefs are involved is to apply Bayes' rule and the concept of perfect Bayesian equilibrium (PBE), which is defined as a strategy combination consisting of best responses such that beliefs follow Bayes' rule in the equilibrium path and do not contradict Bayes' rule out of the equilibrium path.[7] The process of finding the perfect Bayesian equilibrium of a game involves an interaction between backwards induction and forward Bayesian inference.[8] Through a process of Bayesian updating, actors alter their beliefs as a game of incomplete information progresses. With each move, an actor updates his or her probability estimates regarding the other player. Each update is based on an assumption that the other actor is following an equilibrium strategy.

Liberalizers' beliefs are referred to as μ_L, such that $\mu_L(r) =$

---

6. All alternatives are summed in this manner. In this case, there are two alternative conditions for B, B, and not B.

7. Also see Tirole 1988 (436–45) and Fudenberg and Tirole 1991 (209–434).

8. It should be noted that a significant problem with the perfect Bayesian equilibrium concept is that it has a tendency to produce many equilibria. Since the PBE concept calls for an examination of beliefs that lie off the equilibrium path, this should not be too surprising. Many game theorists are now seeking refinements to the notion of equilibrium theory. For example, see Kohlberg and Mertens 1986; Cho and Kreps 1987; Banks and Sobel 1987; Fudenberg, Kreps, and Levine 1988; and Dekel and Fudenberg 1990. Unfortunately, no consensus has emerged on which refinement to use. Nevertheless, PBE is a useful concept for understanding games of incomplete information. See Banks 1991 for a nice review of signaling games applied to political science.

μ_L(successful repression). If society organizes, liberalizers update their beliefs about r conditional on society's decision to organize. This conditional probability belief is represented as, $\mu_L(r|\text{soc. organizes})$. Now, applying Bayes' rule, we can calculate the conditional probability that repression is successful given that society has organized, such that

$$\mu_L(r|\text{soc. orgn.})$$
$$= \frac{\mu_L(\text{soc. orgn.}|r)\mu_L(r)}{\mu_L(\text{soc. orgn.}|r)\mu_L(r) + \mu_L(\text{soc. orgn.}|1-r)\mu_L(1-r)}. \qquad (5.3)$$

To apply Bayes' Theorem to this game and to calculate $\mu_L(r|\text{soc. organizes})$, we need the values of $\mu_L(\text{soc. organizes}|r)$ and $\mu_L(\text{soc. organizes}|1-r)$. From backwards induction we know that the conditional probability of society organizing given successful repression (r) is 0.0; society will not organize if it knows that repression is successful. On the other hand, society will organize with a probability of 1.0 if it knows that repression will be unsuccessful. Plugging this value into Bayes' Theorem, we get

$$\mu_L(r|\text{soc. organizes}) = \frac{r(0)}{r(0) + (1-r)(1)} = 0.0. \qquad (5.4)$$

What does this 0.0 mean?[9] It means that if liberalizers see civil society organize politically, they will alter their beliefs about the value of r down to 0.0. In other words, if society organizes, liberalizers will believe that the chance of successfully repressing society is 0.0. In response they will opt for reform rather than repression. To look at the other side of the story, what happens to the liberalizers' beliefs about r if society enters into a broad dictatorship? This time we need to know the conditional probability of society entering given successful repression; if society knows that repression will be successful, it will enter into a broad dictatorship with a conditional probability of 1.0. Following the same reasoning, society will not enter a broad dictatorship if it knows that repression will be unsuccessful; the conditional probability of society entering given successful repression is 0.0. Plugging these values into Bayes' Theorem we see that

$$\mu_L(r|\text{soc. enters}) = \frac{r(1.0)}{r(1.0) + (1-r)(0.0)} = 1.0. \qquad (5.5)$$

---

9. Recall that, if $r = 0.5$, liberalizers are indifferent between repression and reform. If we set the prior belief about the value of r at the level where liberalizers would be indifferent between repression and reform (0.5), it would make no difference since the conditional probability is 0.

This demonstrates that, if society enters into a broad dictatorship, liberalizers do not alter their priors about the value of r.

What is to be learned from this exercise? First we provided a more rigorous framework for analyzing Przeworski's game. We have offered a payoff ordering for civil society so that we may actually solve for the equilibria of these games. (Przeworski only provides a payoff ordering for one player, the liberalizers.) Through this more rigorous analysis, we have also explicitly incorporated incomplete information into our analysis. In this way, we have exploited the advantages of game theory, namely, its explicit assumptions, rigorous analysis, and clear conclusions. Moreover, from this exercise we also learned that Przeworski's intuition is right, maybe even understated. If society organizes, the liberalizers will not choose repression since they believe such an action will be unsuccessful. It should also be pointed out that the actual value of r does not have to change; only beliefs about r need to change. In this way, beliefs play a central role in building a reputation. We will discuss the role of reputation in political reform in much greater detail in chapter 6. In the next section of this chapter we extend Przeworski's models, using the concept of incomplete information. We examine how uncertainty can play a role in the strategic process of regime transformation.

Alternative Models of Political Liberalization

Two Types of Liberalizers

In Przeworski's models of political liberalization, both players possess complete certainty about the other's type of orientation. Civil society, for example, knows that liberalizers favor broad dictatorship (BDIC) over strong dictatorship (SDIC); this, after all, is what distinguishes them as liberalizers. Incomplete information affects players' assessment of the success of repression, but not actors' preferences. Przeworski presents several alternative games to model variations in liberal preferences. Each game portrays the strategic interaction between civil society and a different type of liberalizer; these are seen in figures 15–17. What happens if civil society does not know what type of liberalizers it faces? Given that these games model aggregated actors, such uncertainty seems quite likely. These actors are actually groups, which would make it difficult to determine what type of player one is facing. In this section, we extend Przeworski's analysis by presenting some alternative models that account for this kind of incomplete information. Such an extension more closely reflects the actual politics of reform, in which actors face considerable uncertainty.

We start with a game involving civil society playing against liberalizers who exhibit preference orderings that reflect the games played in figures 15 and 16. These two games are combined into a single game of incomplete information, which is portrayed in figure 18. In this game liberalizers come in two types, those more and less committed to reform. Nature is used to model in the extensive form whether liberalizers are more committed or less committed to reform. Nature moves first, determining the payoffs associated with different outcomes. Liberalizers make the next choice with complete information about their type. This makes this an asymmetric game. As far as the liberalizers are concerned, Nature dictates the type of game they are playing. Once nature moves, liberalizers make decisions as in the games described in figures 15 and 16. Civil society, however, makes its decision not knowing what type of liberalizers it faces. The game can be summarized as follows.

1. Nature determines a type of liberalizer from a set of types, $t_i \in T$, where $T = \{x,y\}$, where $x = less$ committed to reform and $y = more$ committed to reform. Type t is drawn with a probability distribution of $\theta(t_i)$, where $\theta(t_i) > 0$ and $\theta(T) = 1$.

2. Liberalizers observe t_i and then choose an action, a_L, from the feasible set A_L, where $A_L = \{stay\ with\ hardliners,\ open\}$, and where *stay with hardliners* ends the game, providing the payoffs to both players associated with the outcomes of $SDIC_x$ and $SDIC_y$, where $SDIC_x$ and $SDIC_y$ are outcomes of SDIC contingent on whether Nature has chosen x or y as the type of liberalizer.

3. Civil society observes the liberalizers' choice under incomplete information. If the liberalizers choose *open* then civil society chooses an action, a_{CS}, from the feasible set $A_{CS} = \{enter,\ organize\}$, where *enter* ends the game with the payoffs to both players associated with the $BDIC_x$ and $BDIC_y$ outcomes, depending on whether Nature has chosen x or y. Civil society, making a decision with incomplete information, utilizes Bayes' rule to update its beliefs (μ_{CS}) about the liberalizers' type.

4. If the preceding choices were *open* and *organize*, liberalizers choose either *repress* or *turn into reformers*, where *turn into reformers* ends the game with the payoffs to both players

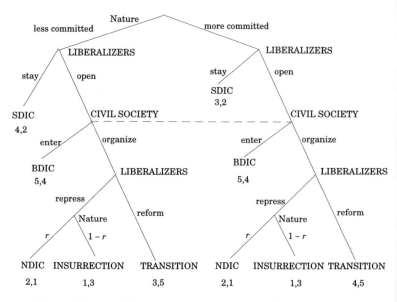

Fig. 18. Przeworski's game with incomplete information. (Data provided by the authors, adapted from Przeworski 1991, 62.)

associated with Transition$_x$ and Transition$_y$, depending on whether Nature chose x or y.

5. If the preceding choices were *open, organize,* and *repress,* Nature determines the payoffs for both players associated with the outcomes, NDIC$_x$, NDIC$_y$, Insurrection$_x$, and Insurrection$_y$, and the game ends.

To analyze this game we begin as before with backwards induction starting at the bottom of the game tree. We start with the final decision node of the liberalizers. From either of the final liberalizer decision nodes, transition is preferred to either narrow dictatorship (NDIC) or Insurrection on both branches of the game tree. Liberalizers possess a dominant strategy to reform.

Now move backward up the game tree to the civil society decision nodes. These two decision nodes are connected by a dotted line representing an information set, meaning that civil society does not know from which node it must make its decision. It makes its decision with incomplete information since it does not know the payoffs associated with different decisions. Given that liberalizers have a dominant strategy to reform, preferring transformation over either Insurrection or narrow dictatorship (NDIC), civil society, in turn, has a dominant strategy to organize. Nature, at this point, does not alter society's choice. Move up the game tree to the initial decision made by the liberalizers; here the liberalizers know their payoffs for different choices. The game possesses asymmetric information; liberalizers possess complete and perfect information while society must operate with incomplete information. Knowing their payoffs, the liberalizers make different choices at different decision nodes. At the left-hand node (being less committed to reform), liberalizers choose to remain hard nosed, preferring strong dictatorship (SDIC) to Transition. At the right-hand node (being more committed to reform), liberalizers choose to open up the political process, preferring Transition to strong dictatorship (SDIC). We see two cases for equilibrium.

> Case 1: {(*stay with hardliners, reform*), *organize*}. This equilibrium exists if Nature determines liberalizers to be less committed.
>
> Case 2: {(*open, reform*), *organize*}. This equilibrium exists if Nature determines liberalizers to be more committed.

Three Types of Liberalizers

We now turn to a game in which Nature determines three types of liberalizers. This game integrates the three types of liberalizers described by Przeworski, represented in figures 15–17. We designate these types of liberalizers as x, y, and z, respectively. This game is presented in extensive form in figure 19. As with the game represented in figure 18, this game is characterized by asymmetric information, where the liberalizers possess complete and perfect information and civil society must make a decision with incomplete information. The game can be summarized as follows.

1. Nature determines a type of liberalizer from a set of types, $t_i \in T$, where $T = \{x,y,z\}$, where x = *less* committed to reform, y = *more* committed to reform, and z = affected by the probability of successful repression (the value of r). Type t is drawn with a probability distribution of $\theta(t_i)$, where $\theta(t_i) > 0$ and $\theta(T) = 1$.

2. Liberalizers observe t_i and then choose an action, a_L, from the feasible set A_L, where $A_L = \{stay\ with\ hardliners,\ open\}$ and where *stay with hardliners* ends the game, providing the payoffs to both players associated with the outcomes of $SDIC_x$,

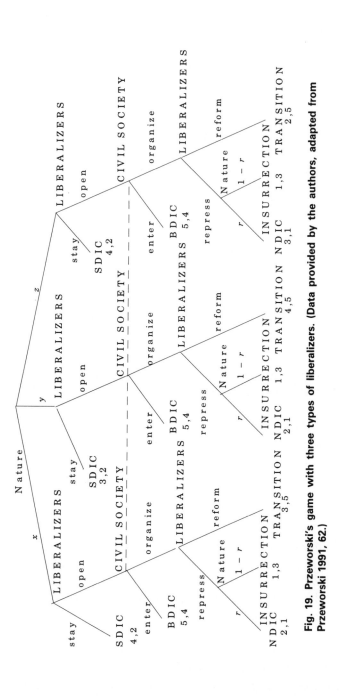

Fig. 19. Przeworski's game with three types of liberalizers. (Data provided by the authors, adapted from Przeworski 1991, 62.)

SDIC$_y$, and SDIC$_z$, where SDIC$_t$ is the outcome of SDIC contingent on whether Nature has chosen x, y, or z as the type of liberalizer.

3. Civil society observes the liberalizers' choice with incomplete information. If the liberalizers choose *open*, then civil society chooses an action, a_{CS}, from the feasible set $A_{CS} = \{enter, organize\}$, where *enter* ends the game with the payoffs to both players associated with the BDIC$_x$, BDIC$_y$, and BDIC$_z$ outcomes, depending on whether Nature chose x, y, or z. Civil society, making a decision with incomplete information utilizes Bayes' rule to update its beliefs (μ_{CS}) about the liberalizers' type.

4. Liberalizers observe civil society's move with incomplete information (but with perfect recall of its own earlier move). If the preceding choices were *open* and *organize*, liberalizers choose either *repress* or *turn into reformers*, where *turn into reformers* ends the game with the payoffs to both players associated with Transition$_x$, Transition$_y$, or Transition$_z$, depending on whether Nature chose x, y, or z.

5. If the preceding choices were *open, organize,* and *repress*, Nature determines the payoffs for both players associated with the outcomes NDIC$_x$, NDIC$_y$, NDIC$_z$, Insurrection$_x$, Insurrection$_y$, or Insurrection$_z$ and the game ends.

To determine the equilibria for this game we again use backwards induction. At the liberalizers' decision nodes at the end of the x and y branches of the game tree, liberalizers have dominant strategies to reform rather than repress, regardless of the value of r. Branch z, however, is different. Under these conditions, the value of r does make a difference. If $r > 0.5$, liberalizers will choose repression over reform. On the other hand, if $r < 0.5$, the chances of successfully repressing political organization are sufficiently low to induce liberalizers to choose reform over repression.

Now move backward up the game tree to society's decision node. Remember, society does not know where it is on the game tree. The best it can do is calculate the probability of being at a particular node. In other words, society attempts to anticipate what type of liberalizers it faces with incomplete information. One way to narrow its choices is to observe what liberalizers have chosen at the first decision node. If Nature chooses x, liberalizers will choose to stay with the hardliners, valuing strong dictatorship (SDIC) more than transformation. If Nature chooses y, liberalizers open the political process; in this case they get a higher payoff from transition than from strong dictatorship. If Nature chooses z, liberalizers will stay with hardliners if $r < 0.5$ and will open up if $r > 0$. If Nature selects x or z, where liberalizers know that $r < 0.5$, the game is over and society has no choice to make. Otherwise, if Nature opts for y or z, where liberalizers know that $r > 0.5$, civil society has a choice because liberalizers will open. If society knew it was on the y branch, it would prefer to organize. If society knew that $r > 0.5$ and that it was on the z branch, it would choose to enter into a broad dictatorship. But society does not know.

How does society make its choice under such conditions of uncertainty? We have shown that, given a choice, civil society knows that nature has selected either y or z, where it is known that $r > 0.5$.[10] If the game is played once with no chance of repetition, civil society will choose between entering and organizing based on its beliefs about the liberalizers' type.

The problem is that civil society in this game does not know what type of liberalizers it faces. Bayes' rule can be used to make a decision under such uncertainty such that

$$\mu_{cs}(t_L|a_L) = \frac{\mu_{cs}(a_L|t_L)\mu_{cs}(t_L)}{\mu_{cs}(a_L|t_L)\mu_{cs}(t_L) + \mu_{cs}(a_L|\neg t_L)\mu_{cs}(\neg t_L)}, \quad (5.6)$$

where $\mu_{cs}(t_L|a_L)$ is the conditional probability that liberalizers will be of type t_L given the action, a_L, taken by the liberalizers, $\mu_{cs}(a_L|t_L)$ is the conditional probability of a_L given t_L, $\mu_{cs}(t_L)$ is the prior belief that t_L would occur, and $\mu_{cs}(a_L|t_L) \mu_{cs}(t_L) + \mu_{cs}(a_L|\neg t_L) \mu_{cs}(\neg t_L)$ is the marginal likelihood of seeing a_L given either t_L or $\neg t_L$ (not t_L).[11] In this game, in which liberalizers know the value of r, civil society knows that if liberalizers make a decision to open up the political process, $r > 0.5$, or they are on the y branch of the game tree. If $r < 0.5$, liberalizers would choose to stay with the hardliners, and the game would be over. Civil society uses Bayes' rule to estimate the probability of the liberalizers being committed to reform, such that

$\mu_{cs}(t_L = y|open)$

$$= \frac{\mu_{cs}(open|t_L = y)\mu_{cs}(t_L = y)}{\mu_{cs}(open|t_L = y)\mu_{cs}(t_L = y) + \mu_{cs}(open|t = z \wedge r > 0.5)\mu_{cs}(t = z \wedge r > 0.5)},$$
$$(5.7)$$

where $\wedge$ signifies the logical expression "and."

---

10. For this example we will assume that only liberalizers know the value of r, particularly whether or not $r >$ or < 0.5. In the next example, we will examine what happens to this game if the value of r is not known by either party.

11. All alternatives are summed in this manner. In this case, there are three alternative conditions for t: x, y, and z.

This calculation of beliefs, in turn, can be used to calculate the expected utilities for entering and organizing. The expected utility of a decision can be calculated by multiplying civil society's beliefs about the type of liberalizers it faces with the payoff associated with being on each respective branch of the game tree. To some extent the liberalizers' decision to *open* signals to civil society what its type is.[12] For example, to obtain the expected utility of politically organizing, civil society multiplies its subjective probability estimate (beliefs) that it is on the *y* branch of the game tree by the payoff of 5 and adds an estimate regarding the probability of being on the *z* branch of the tree and $r = 1$ multiplied by a payoff of 1. (We assume $r = 1$ to simplify our game.) These payoffs are identified through a process of backwards induction. If civil society knows it is on the *y* branch of the game tree, the equilibrium is {(*open, reform*), *organize*}, which is associated with a payoff to civil society of 5. If civil society knows it is on the *z* branch of the game tree and knows $r = 1$, the equilibrium is {(*open, repress*), *organize*}, which is associated with a payoff of 4 for civil society. These calculations can be represented as

$$E_{CS}(organize) = \mu_{cs}(t_L = y | open)(5)$$
$$+ (t_L = z \wedge r > 0.5 | open)(1). \quad (5.8)$$

Similarly, the expected utility of entering into an alliance with the government can be portrayed as

$$E_{CS}(enter) = 4. \quad (5.9)$$

Whether on the *y* or the *z* branch of the game, the liberalizers' move to open up the political process provides a payoff of 4 to civil society if it chooses to enter. Therefore, the expected payoff of entering is 4. Given this information we know that civil society will organize politically if the expected payoff of organizing exceeds the expected payoff of entering into an alliance with the government. Thus, civil society organizes if

$$E_{CS}(organize) > 4. \quad (5.10)$$

If the expected payoff of organizing is less than the expected payoff of entering, civil society will enter into an alliance with the government.

---

12. Przeworski mentions such a signal (1991, 61), but provides no mechanism for incorporating the concept into his analysis. By explicitly incorporating the concepts of incomplete information and perfect Bayesian equilibrium, we can explicitly analyze the role of signals in this game.

Whether the expected payoff of organizing politically is greater or less than the expected payoff of entering is largely determined by the priors assigned to this game. To show how priors affect the expected utility calculation let us make some assumptions about different beliefs and then work through an example.[13] For this example, assume that each branch of the game has almost the same chance of occurring. Keep in mind that civil society does not know the probability associated with each branch of the game tree. Thus, we assume the following beliefs about these probabilities:

$$\mu_{CS}(x) = 0.33,$$

$$\mu_{CS}(y) = 0.33,$$

$$\mu_{CS}(z \wedge r > 0.5) = 0.16,$$

and

$$\mu_{CS}(z \wedge r < 0.5) = 0.16.[14]$$

Given these probabilities, we proportionally set the conditional beliefs as

$$\mu_{CS}(open|y) = 0.66,$$

and

$$\mu_{CS}(open|z \wedge r > 0.5) = 0.34.$$

Plugging these values into the expected utility calculation for organizing we get

$$E_{CS}(organize) = \frac{(0.66)(0.33)}{(0.66)(0.33) + (0.34)(0.16)} (5)$$

$$+ \frac{(0.34)(0.16)}{(0.34)(0.16) + (0.66)(0.33)} (1). \quad (5.11)$$

---

13. Of course, in real life prior beliefs are not given but stem from specific experiences.

14. We assume here that liberalizers will *not* be indifferent between repress and reform.

This simplifies to

$$E_{CS}(organize) = \frac{1.089}{.2722} + \frac{.0544}{.2722} = 4.20. \tag{5.12}$$

Given these priors, the expected payoff from organizing is 4.20; since this is greater than 4, the expected payoff from organizing exceeds the expected payoff from entering. Civil society, in turn, will organize politically. In the more general case, in which priors are not exogenously assumed, civil society will organize when

$$E_{CS}(organize) > E_{CS}(enter).$$

We can also solve for a more general result. Conditional beliefs allow us to set

$$\mu_{CS}(y|open) = 1 - [\mu_{CS}(z \wedge r = 1|open)].$$

Set

$$\mu_{CS}(y|open) = \theta$$

and

$$\mu_{CS}(z \wedge r = 0.5|open) = 1 - \theta.$$

Then the expected payoff of organizing is

$$E_{CS}(organize) = \theta(5) + (1 - \theta)(1).$$

Simplified,

$$E_{CS}(organize) = \theta(4) + 1.$$

Now set the expected payoffs of enter and organize equal to one another to establish the indifference point, such that

$$E_{CS}(enter) = 4 = (4)\theta + 1 = E_{CS}(organize).$$

Solving for θ, it is evident that:

$$\theta = {}^3/_4.$$

Recall that θ equals the belief that the liberalizers' type is y, given a choice of open, that is, $\mu_{CS}(open|y) = \theta$. We now see that $E_{CS}(organize) > E_{CS}(enter)$ when $\theta > 3/4$ and $E_{CS}(enter) > E_{CS}(organize)$ when $\theta < 3/4$. In other words, civil society needs to believe that there is a $3/4$ (75 percent) chance that it is on the y path before organizing, given a decision to open made by liberalizers.

What if $\theta = 3/4$? Then $E_{CS}(enter) = E_{CS}(organize)$ and the equilibria are: $\{(open, reform), (1/2\ enter, 1/2\ organize)\}$ when $t = y$ or $\{(open, repress), (1/2\ enter, 1/2\ organize)\}$ when $t = (z \wedge r > 0.5)$. There are two equilibria because liberalizers know their type and civil society does not, but the mixing is the same, given an indifference between enter and organize. That leads us to ask, what happens if both liberalizers and civil society make their decisions under conditions of uncertainty? What if the game is characterized by two-sided incomplete information?

Two-Sided Incomplete Information

Now we turn to an example in which civil society does not know what type of liberalizer it faces and neither civil society nor the liberalizers know the value of r (the probability of successfully repressing any political organization). The game can be summarized as has been done previously, except in step 4, where the game differs as follows.

4. Liberalizers observe civil society's move with incomplete information (but with perfect recall of their own earlier move). If the preceding choices were *open* and *organize*, liberalizers choose either *repress* or *turn into reformers*, where *turn into reformers* ends the game with the payoffs to both players associated with *Transition_x*, *Transition_y*, or *Transition_z*, depending on whether Nature chose x, y, or z. Liberalizers must make this choice with incomplete information regarding the probability of successful repression (r).

To better understand the role of liberalizers not knowing the value of r, recall equations 5.3, 5.4, and 5.5, wherein liberalizers utilized Bayes' rule to help calculate expected payoffs when r is unknown. In this game we combine elements of equations 5.3 and 5.7, wherein neither liberalizers nor civil society possess complete information. Let us begin with the liberalizers' beliefs. We assume that liberalizers know their type. The problem is that they do not know the value of r. Liberalizers must calculate their expected payoffs from opening the political process drawing on their beliefs about the chances of successful repression (*r*). Civil society also makes its decision with uncertainty, not knowing the type of liberalizers it faces. This turns out to be an unusual game in that it exhibits aspects of asymmetric information (regarding the type of liberalizer) and two-sided incomplete information regarding the value of *r*.

To analyze this game we examine a set of possible equilibrium candidates. Drawing from our previous analysis we present three pure strategy and one mixed strategy perfect Bayesian equilibrium candidates. Many other mixed strategy equilibria exist involving civil society's and liberalizers' beliefs about *r* and civil society's beliefs regarding the type of liberalizer they face.[15]

> *Case 1*: {({*stay, reform*), *organize*}. This pure strategy perfect Bayesian equilibrium exists if civil society believes that Nature has determined that the liberalizers are Type *x*. The existence of this equilibrium was demonstrated earlier in this chapter. This equilibrium also exists if civil society believes that Nature has determined that liberalizers are Type *z* and the expected payoff for liberalizers of *staying* exceeds that of *opening*. This takes place when $\mu_{CS}(r < 0.5)$, that is, when civil society believes that Nature has determined that liberalizers are Type *z* and successful repression is unlikely.
>
> *Case 2*: {(*open, repress*), *enter*}. This pure strategy perfect Bayesian equilibrium exists if civil society believes that Nature has determined that liberalizers are Type *z* and *r* > 0.5, so that liberalizers' expected payoff from *opening* the political process exceeds the expected payoff from *staying* with the hardliners. We are assuming common knowledge regarding the value of *r*. This means that we are assuming that both players believe that *r* possesses the same value.
>
> *Case 3*: {(*open, reform*), *organize*}. This pure strategy perfect Bayesian equilibrium exists if civil society believes that Nature has determined that liberalizers are Type *y* (those most likely to favor political reform and transition). The existence of this equilibrium was demonstrated earlier in this chapter.
>
> *Case 4*: (mixed strategy equilibrium) {(*open*, (²/₃ *open*, ¹/₃ *repress*)), (¹/₃ *organize*, ²/₃ *enter*)}. This mixed strategy perfect

---

15. Any situation involving civil society's belief that they are on the *z* path results in the civil society possessing beliefs about the liberalizers' beliefs about *r*. Situations involving beliefs about beliefs are often referred to as common knowledge problems. We, however, will not elaborate on issues of common knowledge here.

Bayesian equilibrium exists if civil society believes that Nature has determined that liberalizers are type z and that liberalizers believe that $r = 0.5$. Keep in mind that liberalizers know that they are on the z path. This mixed strategy equilibrium was determined in *Case 3* of our version of Przeworski's game depicted in figure 17. Many other mixed strategy equilibria also exist regarding uncertainty about the type of liberalizers civil society faces (y or z) and beliefs about r.

Information obviously plays a role in the analysis of these games. What players know and what they do not know profoundly affects their decisions, which in turn affect the equilibria of these games. By using the analytical concept of information we are also able to combine the variety of games discussed by Przeworski. We have demonstrated that when civil society does not know the type of liberalizers it faces, beliefs become important to such strategic interactions. In the real world of political liberalization, doubts about what type of liberalizers they face within the government are going to significantly affect the behavior of members of civil society.

Reputation: Repeated Games with Incomplete Information

One important way to manipulate an adversary's beliefs is to develop a reputation. This process of reputation building is an important aspect of these games. When a player lacks complete information, he or she must rely on beliefs when making a decision. This is particularly important in games played over a period of time. As such a game progresses, a player, such as the liberalizers, presumably discloses information (his or her probability distribution regarding the propensity to push for reform) through the moves the player makes.[16] With the revelation of this information, civil society will alter its beliefs and may change its moves in response to this revealed information. What one player believes about another can be manipulated very easily, however. By taking "irrational" actions, liberalizers can lead civil society to come to the wrong conclusion about its true propensity for moving toward democratic transition. In other words, an actor manipulates the beliefs of another by making moves that work to establish a reputation.

Now it should be noted that Przeworski argues against modeling

---

16. Or, in game theoretic terms, its type.

democratic transition as a repeated game. This is quite evident in his statement:

> But I do not think that situations in which regime change is at stake are repeatable. These are unique situations. . . . Once Reformers decide to make a move *alea iacta est*—they cannot go back to the status quo. Payoffs for the future change as a result of the actions chosen now. (1991, 72)

Despite Przeworski's claim to the contrary, it is possible to develop a game theoretic model of political liberalization that maintains the spirit of his statement but is technically a repeated game. Theoretically this is done as follows. Take the one-round game presented in figure 19. With regard to the previous three games, as long as liberalizers choose *stay with the hardliners* the game ends and can be repeated; nothing has changed in society. Choosing to stay with the hardliners in effect means maintaining the status quo. A decision to *open*, on the other hand, changes the political system to such an extent that the game is permanently altered. In this section we consider such a repeated game, in which all rounds of the game having an outcome of SDIC lead to a new round of the game with the same payoff structure. All other outcomes end the game with no further repetitions. This game can be summarized as follows.

1. Nature determines a type of liberalizer from a set of types, $t_i \in T$, where $T = \{x,y,z\}$, where $x = less$ committed to reform, $y = more$ committed to reform, and $z =$ affected by the probability of successful repression (the value of r). Type t_i is drawn with a probability distribution of $\theta(t_i)$, where $\theta(t_i) > 0$ and $\theta(T) = 1$.
2. Liberalizers observe t_i and then choose an action, a_L, from the feasible set A_L, and where $A_L = \{stay\ with\ hardliners,\ open\}$ and where *stay with hardliners* leads to the next round of the game, starting again with Nature's determination of the liberalizers' type. This game is repeated K rounds such that no player knows when the Kth round will occur. (This holds except when liberalizers choose to *open* and then later choose to *reform*. As such, there is an end that can be predicted given liberalizer's actions.)[17]
3. Civil society observes the liberalizers' choice with incomplete

---

17. The relevance of such conditional probabilities is examined earlier in this chapter.

information. If the liberalizers choose *open*, then civil society chooses an action, a_{cs}, from the feasible set A_{cs} = {*enter*, *organize*}, where *enter* ends the game with the payoffs to both players associated with the $BDIC_x$, $BDIC_y$, and $BDIC_z$ outcomes, depending on whether Nature chose x, y, or z. Civil society, making a decision with incomplete information, utilizes Bayes' rule to update its beliefs (μ_{cs}) about the liberalizers' type.

4. Liberalizers observe civil society's move with incomplete information (but with perfect recall of their own earlier move). If the preceding choices were *open* and *organize*, liberalizers choose either *repress* or *turn into reformers*, where *turn into reformers* ends the game with the payoffs to both players associated with $Transition_x$, $Transition_y$, or $Transition_z$, depending on whether Nature chose x, y, or z. Liberalizers must make this choice with incomplete information regarding the probability of successful repression (r).

5. If the preceding choices were *open*, *organize*, and *repress*, Nature determines the payoffs for both players associated with the outcomes, $NDIC_x$, $NDIC_y$, $NDIC_z$, $Insurrection_x$, $Insurrection_y$, or $Insurrection_z$, and the game ends.

How does repeating this game in this manner change things? Due to the characteristics of the game, civil society gets no choice if liberalizers stay with the hardliners. If liberalizers open the political process, civil society knows that either liberalizers are on the y branch or the z branch of the game, where $r > 0.5$. In such a repeated environment, the liberalizers' actions signal their type (x, y, or z) each round of the game. This game is characterized by a semiseparating equilibrium such that the actions taken by the liberalizers do not fully identify their type.[18] A hybrid or semiseparating equilibrium operates in the environment in which liberalizers and civil society play a repeated game where choices between *open* and *stay with hardliners* and *organize* and *enter* are randomized; thus the hybrid equilibrium. The posterior beliefs are then $\mu_{CS}(t = z|open) \in (0,\omega)$, $\mu_{CS}(t = y|open) = 1$, and $\mu_{CS}(t = x|open) = 0$. Given this equilibrium, repeating the game plays an important role. Since a choice of staying with the hardliners only leads to another round of the game, the equilibria for this game are as follows.

---

18. We do not mean to imply that all rounds of the political liberalization game possess a separating equilibrium.

Case 1: {(*open, reform*), *organize*}, when civil society believes that it is on the *y* path.

Case 2: {(*open, repress*), *enter*}, when civil society believes it is on the *z* path and $r > 0.5$.

Case 3: {(*stay, reform*), *organize*} when liberalizers are on the *z* path and believe that $r < 0.5$.

Case 4: {(*stay, reform*), *organize*} when liberalizers are on the *x* path.

Case 5: {a set of mixed strategies of *open* and *enter*, and a set of mixed strategies of *repress* and *reform*}.

The implication is that repeating the game does not have significant implications beyond the changes that result from incomplete information.

Summary

So, how has the analysis presented in this chapter contributed to Przeworski's work? The most elementary contribution was to specify civil society's payoffs. Przeworski alludes to these preferences in his text, but nowhere does he directly incorporate them into his analysis; he only specifies the payoff ordering for the liberalizers. With this change we are able to provide a more rigorous analysis of Przeworski's games and any variations that we subsequently develop. The second part of the chapter examines situations in which civil society faces liberalizers whose type is unknown to it. Such a scenario more accurately reflects actual situations of political liberalization. Such an analysis allows us to integrate several of Przeworski's games into one game. He alludes to such an integration in his text but never attempts such an analysis. We provide several variations here, varying the amount of information various actors possess. Finally, this analysis also allows us to demonstrate the implications of incomplete information and the role of beliefs in these games. Uncertainty is pervasive in the political world. This chapter provides a perspective on the role of information and beliefs on strategic behavior and outcomes.

CHAPTER 6

Commitment, Bluffs, and Reputation

Any poker player will tell you that bluffing is an essential element of strategy. Bluffing is also important in strategic political interactions. When we bluff we manipulate an adversary's beliefs. As was demonstrated in the previous chapter, any player lacking complete information must rely on beliefs when making a decision. When a game is played over time, these beliefs can be updated. As such a game progresses a player discloses information about its probability of making a particular choice through the moves he or she makes. In game theoretic terms, we say that one *type* of player is more likely to make a certain choice than is another type of player. As players move, they presumably reveal what types of players they are. Beliefs about another player, however, can be manipulated easily. "Irrational" actions can lead another player to the wrong conclusion about what type of player he or she faces. In other words, reputation is used to manipulate the beliefs of another. In this chapter we feature the role of incomplete information in repeated games, examining bluffing, commitment, and reputation.

Chapter 3 served to differentiate game theory from decision theory using Rohde's model of strategic ambition. Chapter 4 distinguished between perfect and imperfect information using Conybeare's models of trade wars. In this chapter we return to the strategic model of progressive ambition and Conybeare's Asymmetric Trade game, presenting more fully explicated models that account for incomplete information. Modeling the strategic interaction between a challenger and an incumbent with incomplete information provides a richer understanding of strategic ambition. In this chapter we also introduce the sanction game to examine the politics of commitment. Examining the Asymmetric Trade game in an environment of incomplete information with repeated play, we can appreciate the role that bluffing and commitment can play in international politics.

The Chain Store game has been examined from a variety of perspectives to provide insights for understanding the role of reputation. Many political scientists are familiar with the Chain Store paradox (Selten 1978). In Selten's original game, decisions are made in an environment of complete and perfect information. The game involves a chain store (M) with branches in 20 towns. In each of these towns there is a potential competitor, k (where $k \in \{1, 2, \ldots 20\}$), who decides whether or not to enter the market. This entry decision is represented in the first decision node in one play of the extensive game presented in figure 20. If the potential competitor actually enters the market, the chain store monopolist can respond either aggressively or cooperatively (seen in the second decision node in figure 20). The game proceeds in the same fashion for all 20 potential competitors.

Using backwards induction, Selten determined that responding aggressively to potential entrants is precluded by rational behavior with complete and perfect information. In fact, the nonaggressive response is a subgame perfect equilibrium.[1] Given the payoffs in the final period, Player 20 will maximize her payoffs by entering the market; the chain store's corresponding decision is to play cooperatively and not try to drive away the competition through predatory pricing.[2] Working backward, the same decisions hold for all periods of play. The equilibrium point for the chain store occurs when a cooperative strategy is selected; this outcome, however, runs counter to intuition. Selten contends that a paradox exists since a chain store could deter entry by sanctioning early in the game to establish reputation effects. Thus, he argues that it makes more sense for the chain store to play tough in the initial periods of the game to deter the entry of additional competitors in the future. This is a solution contrary to the one produced through game theoretic analysis. This divergence between the intuitively derived best strategy and the subgame perfect equilibrium is the source of the paradox. Selten's solution to this paradox suggests a limited rationality view of decision making.

Kreps and Wilson (1982) and Milgrom and Roberts (1982) provide ways to resolve the Chain Store paradox by examining the game under conditions of incomplete or asymmetric information. As has been shown, if entrants (k) possess perfect information, a rational monopolist (M) never responds aggressively to market entry; however, if entrants lack complete information, incumbent monopolists (M) may select an aggressive strategy to deter subsequent market entry. Milgrom and Roberts assume that entrants have doubts about the alternatives available to the monopolist. Potential competitors thus

---

1. In equilibrium, no player has an incentive to alter a chosen strategy. Under perfect equilibrium, the equilibrium holds for all subgames of a supergame. A more complete discussion of subgame perfect equilibrium can be found in chapter 2.

2. Predatory pricing occurs when a firm cuts prices to drive other firms out of the industry or to deter entry.

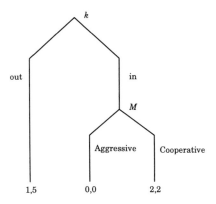

Fig. 20. Selten's Chain Store game. (From Selten 1978, 129. Reproduced with kind permission from Kluwer Academic Publishers.)

perceive that the monopolist may only be able to retaliate. For example, a monopolist may not be a unitary rational actor and may be locked into an aggressive response strategy due to some set of factors affecting individuals within the firm. The source of the monopolist's decision, however, is not the issue; what is relevant is the entrant's doubt about whether the monopolist will respond cooperatively or aggressively. It is this uncertainty that may deter market entry. Figure 21 provides a simplified representation of the Milgrom and Roberts game, in which Nature dictates whether or not the monopolist (M) can only respond aggressively.[3]

Kreps and Wilson also consider the role of incomplete information. Rather than focusing on the available alternatives, they examine the payoffs of the incumbent firm. In this situation, the chain store is either strong or weak. A weak monopolist faces the same payoffs as in Selten's game; a strong monopolist, on the other hand, obtains a higher payoff from responding aggressively to market entry than from cooperating (even in the short run). This difference can be seen in a simplified version of this game in figure 22[4] in which Nature determines whether a chain store (M) is strong or weak. A strong firm is shown to obtain a payoff of 2 for an aggressive strategy as opposed to 0 for a cooperative strategy; with a weak monopolist, cooperation provides a payoff of 2, while aggressive behavior is a worse alternative, giving a payoff of 0. Entrants in this situation lack the complete information needed to determine whether the incumbent is a strong or weak chain store. This uncertainty, in turn, may serve to deter market

3. This figure is similar to one found in Trockel 1986 (163–79).
4. Again, see Trockel 1986.

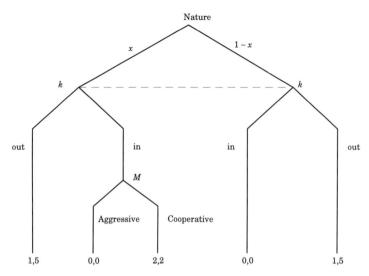

Fig. 21. Milgrom and Roberts' entry deterrence game. (From Trockel 1986, 168. Reproduced with kind permission from Kluwer Academic Publishers.)

entry. As long as this uncertainty exists, it becomes rational for even a weak monopolist to play aggressively to establish a strong chain store reputation early in the game in order to discourage market entry in the later stages. The long-term benefits of building a reputation through bluffing, then, may outweigh the short-term costs.

The Chain Store game provides insight beyond antitrust policy. The Kreps and Wilson version of the Chain Store game has been applied to political leadership in two very different contexts. Calvert (1987) modifies the game to examine the effect of reputation on legislative leadership. Alt, Calvert, and Humes (1988) apply a version of this game to the international scene by examining hegemonic leadership, specifically drawing on an example from recent developments in the Organization of Petroleum Exporting Countries (OPEC). Also refer to chapter 2, where we applied this model to the conflict between the United States and New Zealand regarding U.S. naval vessels carrying nuclear weapons and the breakdown of ANZUS. In these analyses, unlike those of Kreps and Wilson, costs may vary from one situation to the next. Here the legislative followers (Calvert) and allies of the hegemon (Alt, Calvert, and Humes) take on the role of entrants, choosing to obey or rebel in each period, t, of the game. The legislative leader, or hegemon, in turn, operates in the same manner as does the chain store (M), deciding to either acquiesce or punish a rebellious follower. Followers lack certainty about the payoffs available to a

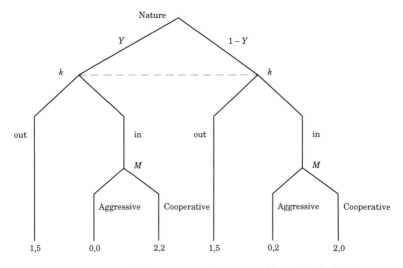

Fig. 22. Kreps and Wilson's entry deterrence. (From Trockel 1986, 168. Reproduced with kind permission from Kluwer Academic Publishers.)

leader and thus can be deterred from rebelling if a leader possesses a reputation for punishing rebels. In these two applications, a model with incomplete information is used to show the role of reputation in developing and maintaining leadership.

Commitment is another significant aspect of reputation. To examine commitment, Trockel (1986) makes another modification of Selten's game. Rather than looking at situations of incomplete information, Trockel examines this game in light of complete but imperfect information. Under conditions of incomplete information, players are uncertain about their opponents' choices since they lack information about the other players' payoffs. With imperfect information, players are unaware of what the other player has done. In a sequential game this can make a big difference. Figure 23 provides a representation of what happens when the choices are reversed with a weak monopolist. Here the monopolist (*M*) decides first whether to cooperate or respond aggressively. If Player *k* decides in ignorance of *M*'s decision, it makes no real difference to the entrant whether she is playing Selten's or Trockel's game. (This lack of information is represented by the information set connecting Player *k*'s decision nodes.) Nevertheless, the monopolist's decision is affected. In this new scenario, the monopolist must decide between cooperation and aggression before knowing whether the potential competitor has chosen in or out. There would be no difference between selecting cooperation or aggression if the potential competitor decides not to enter, since there is no differ-

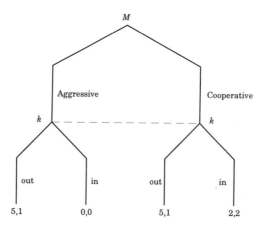

Fig. 23. Trockel's entry deterrence game. (Trockel 1986, 170. Reproduced with kind permission from Kluwer Academic Publishers.)

ence in the consequences. Yet, there is a difference in payoffs if the monopolist chooses a cooperative strategy. Under these conditions, the cooperative (in) path remains a perfect sequential equilibrium, but now the aggressive (out) choice is also a sequential equilibrium. If this game is repeated, a monopolist can develop a reputation for playing aggressively and later entrants will respond by choosing to stay out of the market. Such a strategy does not call into question the rationality of the monopolist but provides an equilibrium outcome.

To summarize, the characteristics of the Chain Store game, both in Selten's (1978) and later variations, are listed below. First, all entry firms are assumed to be essentially identical; the monopolist, therefore, faces little uncertainty. In fact, the potential competitor is the player facing uncertainty regarding the ability of the chain store to impose a sanction without incurring great costs. This, however, is not the case with the Calvert (1987) and the Alt, Calvert, and Humes (1988) versions of this game, where payoffs to the hegemon change from time to time. Second, the payoffs of the Chain Store games do not change over time; everything is held constant. Again, this is not the case with either Calvert or Alt, Calvert, and Humes, where payoffs change with different players over time. Third, in the Chain Store game, payoff values emanate from the qualities and capabilities of the monopolist. Under conditions of incomplete information, payoffs change with respect to the capabilities of the incumbent. Kreps and Wilson (1982) make the distinction between strong and weak chain stores. Potential market entrants face an uncertain decision about whether an incumbent is weak or strong. This uncertainty, in turn, can be used by the chain store in responding to entry; hence, a weak firm can establish a reputation by acting as though it were strong and cost effectively able to sanction a market entrant. Outside of these reputation effects, however, it is the capability to respond to market entry that establishes the payoff levels.

Commitment and International Sanctions

This section concerns when and why dominant nation-states will impose sanctions on other powers. It also concerns the ability of one country to induce policy change in another. In order to address these points, the following questions need to be examined. How do these factors motivate dominant states to impose or not impose sanctions, and what are the costs and benefits associated with such sanctions?

The Sanction game involves several players: a dominant state (D) and the recipients (Players, $k \in \{1, 2, \ldots, m\}$). The game is broken down into a separate period for each actor. The payoffs for a single period are shown below in figure 24 in an extensive form representation of the game. A recipient's best outome occurs when he or she receives the benefits of the relationship with the donor without paying the cost of the policy change. This payoff is represented as b.[5] The next best outcome occurs when a recipient acquiesces to the demands of the donor. In this case, the recipient still receives the benefits of the relationship but must bear the costs of policy reform. This payoff is represented as $b - c$. The worst payoff for the recipient takes place when he or she does not comply with the donor's conditions and is subsequently sanctioned. This payoff is designated as $-d$. The donor's most preferred outcome occurs when the recipient complies with the conditions and alters his or her policy. This payoff is represented as b. The worst outcome for the donor takes place when the recipient does not comply and the donor imposes sanctions. The cost of this penalty to the donor is $-p$. A preference located somewhere between these two outcomes occurs when the recipient does not comply and the donor acquiesces. Since the donor avoids the costs of imposing a sanction, this payoff is 0 for the donor. This game is then repeated for each player. Thus, the single play game is part of a time dependent supergame. The game proceeds as follows.

---

5. The use of algebraic payoffs is preferred to the use of cardinal numbers. We know the preference ordering; we do not know how much more one outcome is valued than another except by assumption. In this way, algebraic payoffs are more general. We presented numerical payoffs earlier because they are easier for the reader to follow.

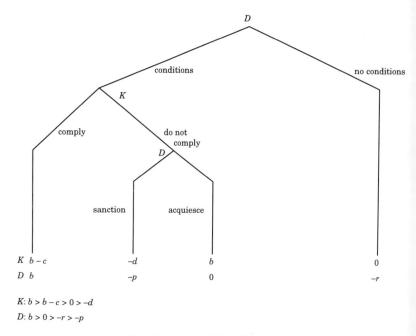

$K: b > b - c > 0 > -d$
$D: b > 0 > -r > -p$

Fig. 24. The conditionality game

1. In period t, Player D first decides whether or not to impose a set of policy conditions designed to induce policy reform in the recipient country, $k \in \{1, \ldots, m\}$. Thus, D chooses an action, a_D, from the feasible set, A_D, where $A_D = \{specify\ conditions,\ no\ conditions\}$. If there is a decision not to impose conditions for policy reform, neither player makes a move during the remainder of this period, providing payoffs of $(0,0)$. On the other hand, if Player D announces a decision to impose conditions for policy reform, the game continues.

2. Given a decision to *specify conditions* by Player D, Player k chooses an action, a_k, from the feasible set $A_k = \{comply,\ do\ not\ comply\}$, where comply provides a payoff of $(b,\ b - c)$ for the period. If the recipient accepts the terms of conditionality, the dominant state, D, has no reason to respond with sanctions, and the game ends for this round.

3. If Player k chooses *not to comply*, D then must decide whether or not to impose sanctions; if Player k opts for compliance, no sanction decision is needed from Player D. The payoffs are $(-p,\ -d)$ if sanctions are chosen, $(0,\ b)$ if they are not.

Given the structure of the Sanction game, equilibrium for each period of the game lies along a path whereby conditions for policy reform are specified by D, the recipient of these conditions does not comply with these policy reforms, and D responds by not sanctioning the noncompliant aid recipient {(*specify conditions, acquiesce*), *do not comply*}.

As with the Chain Store game, the outcome of Sanction is paradoxical. Player D ought to be able to do better by being tough initially, but he or she does not. By sanctioning the first recalcitrant recipients, D could deter further noncompliance. When noncompliant recipients are not sanctioned, future recipients are more likely to view continuing to pursue controversial policies to be relatively risk free. In this manner, the effect is not limited to future plays with recipient k, but is extended to other recipients as well. For the most part, this aspect of the Sanction game is borne out empirically. The cases in which sanctions were implemented are regarded as exceptional. What is found is that, despite following a utility maximizing strategy, a dominant state playing the Sanction game finds that such a strategy does not lead to an optimal outcome.

Essentially this is a problem of "dynamic inconsistency," whereby selecting a decision that is best for the current situation is suboptimal in the long run. For the Sanction game, the problem from D's perspective is not with a particular decision not to sanction but the effect of such a choice on other recipients. Facing a noncompliant recipient, a dominant state encounters a broad strategic choice. Should D follow a reactive or firmly committed strategy?

A reactive strategy essentially is a decision made to satisfy short-term interests that runs counter to a choice to maximize long-term returns. Individuals face this dilemma regularly. After making a resolution to start dieting, the reactive decision maker violates the resolution by taking a third helping of pie and ice cream. These backsliders realize that such choices are not optimal, but they are maximizing in the short run. The trick used by Ulysses facing the Sirens, as well as most dieters, is to prevent oneself from following a reactive decision path.[6] Such techniques of binding involve an actor making a decision at time t to increase the probability that another choice will be made at time t. In the case of international sanctions, a dominant state following a committed strategy essentially makes its choice before the recipient does.

Up to this point, the Sanction game has portrayed D as a reactive decision maker. In most cases, D chooses not to implement costly sanctions, thereby opting to maximize payoffs for one round of the Sanction game rather than over the long run. Figure 25 serves to focus

---

6. See Elster 1984, Schelling 1980, and Gates 1989.

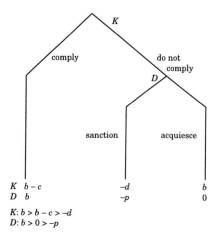

K: $b > b - c > -d$
D: $b > 0 > -p$

Fig. 25. A reduced form of the conditionality game

attention on the reactive nature of D's strategy. This figure portrays one round of this part of the Sanction game. It is important to note that many such games proceed in parallel, involving numerous recipients. In a single round of the game, after the recipient has not complied with the conditionality agreement, D must choose whether or not to sanction the noncompliant recipient. Given a reactive strategy, D is completely responsive to the immediate circumstances. D chooses to maximize $U(k,d)$ such that $d = D(k)$. Given that the recipient decides whether or not to comply before D decides whether or not to sanction, the recipient opts for i in order to maximize $U(k,D(k))$. For the Sanction game this means that recipients will choose noncompliance and D reacts by not imposing costly sanctions.

Under a committed strategy, D could alter this outcome. Figure 26 diagrammatically demonstrates this point. This figure reflects the one developed by Trockel (1986) as presented in figure 23. A dominant state, D, that can commit itself to sanctioning a noncompliant recipient before the recipient can successfully deter such a decision. Essentially, D commits to d before the recipient chooses. In this manner, the recipient chooses to maximize $U(k,d)$ such that $k = K(d)$. D commits to a choice of d to maximize $U(K(d),d)$. In figure 26, the recipient is shown to make its choice after D but in ignorance of D's decision. This is represented by the information set connecting Player k's decision node. The recipient thus makes its decision under complete but imperfect information. This means that a committed D is able to deter recipients from noncompliance.

Reputation plays a key role for both the recipient and the domi-

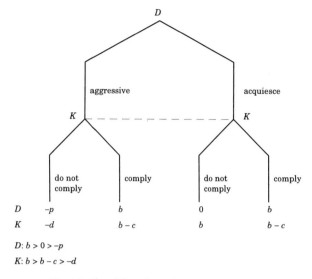

D: $b > 0 > -p$
K: $b > b - c > -d$

Fig. 26. Conditionality with commitment

nant state. While dominant states have a difficult time appraising compliance, they do have a pretty good idea about a recipient's record of compliance in previous years; if a recipient develops a reputation for never complying with any conditions, a dominant state interested in imposing sanctions may determine that it is not worth attempting to induce policy reform. Sanctioning countries do not know if a recipient is going to comply with a particular condition but can use previous actions as an indicator of future actions. In many respects, a sanctioning state's use of this reputation information is analogous to what economists refer to as a signal.[7] A signal essentially serves to convey otherwise unobservable information; in this way previous actions are used to convey information about future decisions.

Reputation information is used by recipients as well as dominant states. Powers that tend to follow reactive strategies develop a reputation for not sanctioning noncompliant recipients. Such a reputation can be very costly, since no recipient is likely to be deterred by a dominant state with a reputation for not sanctioning. This, in a nutshell, is the cost involved in following a short-run, maximizing, reactive strategy.

Given the temptation of the short-run reward of a reactive strategy, institutional devices are developed to limit or discourage such choices. Without such devices, a committed strategy will be rare.

7. See Banks 1991 for applications of signaling games to politics.

These mechanisms essentially work by increasing the cost of reactiveness. Such attempts include limiting decision latitude or directly reducing the payoffs of a reactive choice before the decision is made. In other words, a decision is made ex ante to reduce the payoffs of a reactive strategy ex post.

Laws serve as one method of limiting decision latitude to improve commitment. Laws can restrict the actions of future decision makers. For example, the U.S. Congress has passed legislation that commits the U.S. Agency for International Development (USAID) to particular actions. In particular, USAID is committed to sanctioning aid recipients found to be insufficiently restraining the trafficking of illegal narcotics or pursuing the development of nuclear weapons capabilities. Such laws, of course, can also be repealed; however, regularly repealing laws is costly. Nevertheless, the U.S. Congress has repealed such laws. One such case involved the development of nuclear weapons capabilities in Pakistan (Gates 1989). Legal restrictions can limit the reactiveness of bilateral foreign assistance donors and insure that noncompliant recipients are sanctioned; such arrangements, however, are not as applicable for multilateral institutions.

Note that the law restricts the dominant state. It does not limit the recipient's ability to not comply with conditions specified by the dominant state. Contracts can never specify all contingencies and are unenforceable among sovereign states. The covenants of a conditionality agreement essentially are contracts; yet, as with many international agreements, they are without legal authority. Dominant states must rely on sanctioning noncompliant recipients themselves.

The other technique for avoiding the problems of a reactive strategy is to reduce the costs of commitment. For the Sanction game this involves diminishing the costs of imposing sanctions on noncompliant recipients. By altering these costs, the relative payoffs from a reactive choice are reduced, thereby making a reactive strategy less tempting. The problem is that there are few mechanisms by which a power can reduce the costs of commitment.

The important question is which is more important, maintaining the international relationship or inducing policy change. If policy reforms are more highly valued by a dominant state, a committed strategy should be pursued. Alternatively, if maintaining the international relationship (e.g., continuing to give foreign aid or maintaining most-favored-nation trade status) is more important than the policy reforms prescribed by conditionality, then the costs of foregoing aid make sanctioning too costly even in the long run. Things are seldom so easy, however. Global powers often want both the benefits from the relationship and the reforms that come with policy reform. This dilemma basically comes down to a question of the value of policy reform.

Progressive Ambition with Incomplete Information

In chapter 3, we argued that Rohde's approach to studying progressive ambition was problematic since he used a decision theoretic, as opposed to game theoretic, framework. We then developed two simple game theoretic models involving the choices of a challenger and an incumbent in deciding whether or not to run for the same office. One model considered the case of a strong incumbent and the other the case of a strong challenger. Both games assumed that the choices of the candidates occurred simultaneously. In this section, a more complicated model is developed. Using the techniques developed in the previous chapters, we develop a game of incomplete information that represents the choices faced by an incumbent and a potential challenger.

This game is presented in figure 27. In this game, Nature moves first. With a probability of α the incumbent is stronger electorally than is the challenger (A). With a probability of $1 - \alpha$, the incumbent is weaker than the challenger (B). While the value of α is known to both the incumbent and the challenger, the actual choice of Nature is only revealed to the incumbent. The challenger does not know if she is facing a strong or a weak incumbent. After Nature moves, the incumbent must decide whether to retire (R_t) or run again (R_n). After making this choice, the challenger must then decide whether to stay with her present office (S_t) or run for the incumbent's elected office (E_n). This decision is made with knowledge of the actions of the incumbent but without knowledge of Nature's choice, that is, the incumbent's type.

What is the equilibrium in this game? Since we are dealing with a game of incomplete information, we must search for Bayesian Nash equilibria. As in the example in chapter 2, there are 16 possible combinations of pure strategies. However, these combinations can be summarized in six cases. In the rest of this section, we will develop these cases.

Case (i): The incumbent chooses (a) R_n if Nature chooses A
and (b) R_t if Nature chooses B.
The challenger chooses (a) S_t if the incumbent
chooses to R_n
and (b) E_n if the incumbent
chooses to R_t.

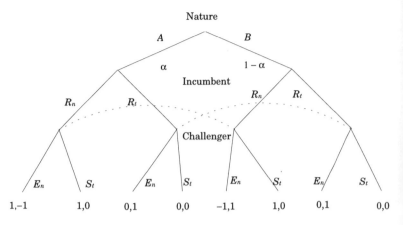

Fig. 27. A model of progressive ambition with incomplete information

This case is not an equilibrium since the incumbent will choose to change his strategy. If the challenger will not challenge the incumbent, the incumbent receives a better payoff by running regardless of Nature's choice. In both possible scenarios, the incumbent increases his payoff from 0 to 1 by choosing R_n instead of R_t.

How should the challenger react to this change in strategy? This case is developed in case (ii).

> *Case (ii):* The incumbent chooses (a) R_n if Nature chooses A
> and (b) R_n if Nature chooses B.
> The challenger chooses (a) S_t if the incumbent
> chooses to R_n
> and (b) E_n if the incumbent
> chooses to R_t.

This case is not as simple to analyze. We need to resort to Bayes' Theorem to consider whether this case is an equilibrium. The probability that the state of Nature is A, given that the incumbent chose R_n, is provided in the following equation:

$$P(A|R_n) = \frac{P(R_n|A)P(A)}{P(R_n|A)P(A) + P(R_n|B)P(B)}.$$

Substituting the appropriate values yields

$$P(A|R_n) = \frac{\alpha}{\alpha + 1 - \alpha}.$$

This probability is then α. Similarly, $P(B|R_n) = 1 - \alpha$.[8] To decide whether the challenger should choose S_t if the incumbent chooses R_n, one must examine the relationship between $E(S_t|R_n)$ and $E(E_n|R_n)$. These values are calculated below.[9]

$$E(S_t|R_n) > E(E_n|R_n)$$
$$\alpha(0) + (1 - \alpha)(0) > \alpha(-1) + 1(1 - \alpha)$$
$$0 > 1 - 2\alpha$$
$$\alpha > 1/2.$$

If α is greater than 0.5, this strategy combination and set of beliefs define a Bayesian Nash equilibrium. This equilibrium is a pooling equilibrium since the incumbent will choose R_n regardless of Nature's choice. If α is less than 0.5, the challenger will change her strategy such that she chooses E_n if the incumbent chooses to R_n. Thus, this strategy combination is only an equilibrium if α is greater than 0.5.

This brings us to our next case.

Case (iii): The incumbent chooses (a) R_n if Nature chooses A
and (b) R_n if Nature chooses B.
The challenger chooses (a) E_n if the incumbent
chooses to R_n
and (b) E_n if the incumbent
chooses to R_t.

This case is not an equilibrium. The incumbent will be better off if he chooses to R_t when Nature chooses B given that the challenger is going to run regardless of the incumbent's choice. By choosing R_n in this case, the incumbent increases his payoff from -1 to 0.

The change in strategy yields our next case, in which the incumbent chooses to R_n if Nature chooses A and chooses to R_t if Nature chooses B, while the challenger chooses E_n regardless of the action of the incumbent.

Case (iv): The incumbent chooses (a) R_n if Nature chooses A
and (b) R_t if Nature chooses B.
The challenger chooses (a) E_n if the incumbent
chooses to R_n
and (b) E_n if the incumbent
chooses to R_t.

---

8. The challenger gains no new information from observing the incumbent's action in this case. The $P(A)$ is equal to the $P(A|R_n)$.

9. We use cardinal utilities here so that the results can be more easily compared with the games presented in chapter 3.

This case is not an equilibrium. The challenger will choose S_t if the incumbent chooses R_n since this yields the challenger 0 instead of -1. In this case, the challenger, realizing that the incumbent is truthfully revealing his type, has no incentive to challenge an incumbent who does not retire. An incumbent who runs for reelection will only be a strong incumbent in this case. Of course, this change does not yield an equilibrium because the incumbent now has an incentive to bluff, as was shown in case (i).

Thus far, we have considered combinations of strategies individually. In dealing with the remaining 12 strategy combinations, we will consider them jointly in the two remaining cases. The first eight are considered in the following case.

Case (v): The incumbent chooses (a) R_t if Nature chooses A.

This case is also not an equilibrium. If Nature chooses A, the incumbent knows that he can defeat the challenger. Why, then, would the incumbent choose to retire? In each of the eight cases of strategy combinations that involve the incumbent retiring if Nature chooses A, he would want to choose instead to run for reelection.

The remaining four possible pure strategy combinations can be examined by using the following case.

Case (vi): The challenger chooses (b) S_t if the Incumbent chooses to R_t.

This case cannot be an equilibrium since the challenger should always run if the incumbent retires. The office is there for the taking. Why, then, would she choose not to run?

In this game, we have identified one perfect Bayesian Nash equilibrium with pure strategies. This arose from case (ii). This equilibrium seems to be a "reasonable" one. It calls for a challenger to refrain from running for the higher office if she believes that there is a greater than 0.5 probability of the incumbent being strong. Alternatively, if the challenger believes that this probability is actually less than 0.5, she will choose to run regardless of the actions of the incumbent. This equilibrium only holds for a certain set of beliefs.

How does this game enhance Rohde's analysis? In this analysis, we have explicitly considered the interaction between the incumbent and a potential challenger. The actions of the incumbent have been shown to depend on those of the challenger and vice versa. In addition, we have considered how subjective beliefs concerning the strength of the challenger and incumbent can affect the outcome of this game. These are all factors Rohde could not consider given his decision theoretic framework.

Asymmetric Trade with Incomplete Information

Bluffing has special relevance in the Asymmetric Trade game. Recall our presentation of Conybeare's Asymmetric Trade game in chapter 4 (portrayed in matrix 18 as a matrix form and in fig. 11 as an extensive form). One could also refer to Asymmetric Trade as a game involving a "predatory hegemon." Does incomplete information make it more tempting for a small country to attempt to deter a large country from defecting (from playing the role of the predator)? Yes, incomplete information does make a difference. Consider the extensive form of the Asymmetric Trade game. With complete and perfect information, a small country will cooperate even when moving first in a sequential choice game to avoid what it regards as the disastrous outcome of mutual defection. As long as there is a final decision node, large countries will always defect, knowing that they can prey on the cooperative small power. With incomplete information, it is possible for a small country to bluff that it is also strong or at least capable of standing up to the large power. Conybeare describes such a situation "where the small country is willing to hurt itself (or credibly threaten to hurt itself) in order to hurt the large country" (1987, 36). See figure 28. As is evident from this game, Nature determines whether the small country, X, is weak or strong. A weak X cannot harm Y, but a strong X can harm Y. Moreover, a large country facing a strong small country will prefer to cooperate while a large country facing a weak small country will prefer to defect. Essentially, this game involves a situation that is characterized either by the Asymmetric Trade game (when X is weak) or the Stag Hunt game (when X is strong). The large country (Y) is uncertain as to which game it is playing.

1. Nature determines the type of the small country (X) from a set of types, $t_i \in T$, where $T = \{weak, strong\}$. Type t is drawn with a probability distribution of $\theta(t_i)$, where $\theta(t_i) > 0$ and $\theta(T) = 1$.
2. Small country X observes t_i and then chooses an action, a_X, from the feasible set A_X, where $A_X = \{defect, cooperate\}$.
3. Large country Y observes small country X's choice under incomplete information and chooses an action, a_Y, from the feasible set $A_Y = \{defect, cooperate\}$. Large country Y, mak-

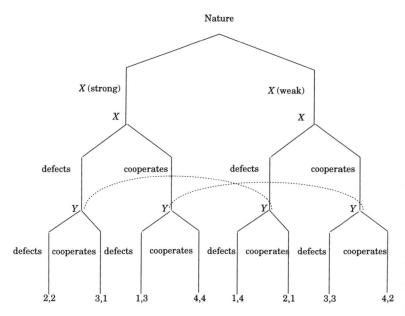

Fig. 28. A variation on Asymmetric Trade

ing a decision with incomplete information, utilizes Bayes' rule to update its beliefs (μ_Y) about small country X's type.
4. Payoffs are given by $U_X(t_i, a_X, a_Y)$ and $U_Y(t_i, a_X, a_Y)$.

To analyze this game we begin as before with backwards induction starting at the bottom of the game tree. We start with the final decision node of the large country Y. At this point the large country will only know whether the small country has defected or cooperated; it will not know whether X is strong or weak. If X defects, Y has a dominant strategy to defect also. Given that X defects, if X is strong, Y will receive a payoff of 2; if X is weak, Y gets a payoff of 3.[10] Despite the differences in payoffs, the decision is the same. The large country Y has a dominant strategy to defect whenever the small country X defects.

The situation is different if the small country X cooperates. Given incomplete information, Y must decide to cooperate or defect contingent upon its beliefs about X's type. If X is strong and X has cooperated, Y gets a payoff of 4 for cooperation and 3 for defection. If X is weak and X has cooperated, Y obtains a payoff of 2 for cooperation and 4 for defection. There is no dominant strategy in this situation.

---

10. We also use cardinal utilities here so that comparisons to chapter 4 and Conybeare's analysis can be made more easily.

Given this problem, in which Y does not know what type of X it faces, Y uses Bayes' rule to make a decision under uncertainty such that:

$$\mu_Y(t = strong|a_X)$$
$$= \frac{\mu_Y(a_X|t = strong)\mu_Y(t = strong)}{\mu_Y(a_X|t = strong)\mu_Y(t = strong) + \mu_Y(a_X|t = weak)\mu_Y(t = weak)},$$

where $\mu_Y(t = strong|a_X)$ is the conditional probability that X will be a strong type given the action, a_X, taken by X, $\mu_Y(a_X|t = strong)$ is the conditional probability of a_X given $t =$ strong, $\mu_Y(t = strong)$ is the prior belief that $t =$ strong would occur, and $\mu_Y(a_X|t = strong)$ $\mu_Y(t = strong) + \mu_Y(a_X|t = weak) \, \mu_Y(t = weak)$ is the marginal likelihood of seeing a_X given either $t =$ strong or $t =$ weak.[11] The strong country Y can use Bayes' rule to estimate the probability of the small country being strong, such that:

$$\mu_Y(t = strong|coop)$$
$$= \frac{\mu_Y(coop|t = strong)\mu_Y(t = strong)}{\mu_y(coop|t = strong)\mu_Y(t = strong) + \mu_Y(coop|t = weak)\mu_Y(t = weak)}.$$

This calculation of beliefs, in turn, can be used to calculate Y's expected utilities for cooperating and defecting. The expected utility of such a decision can be calculated by multiplying Y's beliefs about the type of X it faces with the payoff associated with being on each respective branch of the game tree.

Now move up the game tree to the decision made by the small power X; here X knows its type. The game possesses asymmetric information; liberalizers possess complete and perfect information while society must operate with incomplete information. X also knows that if it defects, Y has a dominant strategy also to defect regardless of whether X is strong or weak. We can see that the best X can achieve if it defects is a payoff of 2 (when X is strong and Y defects); if X is weak, *(defect, defect)* gives X a payoff of 1. Using backwards induction we can compare the payoffs from defection with those from cooperation. If X cooperates, the worst it can do is get a payoff of 2 (when Y defects and X is weak).

To analyze this game, we examine a set of four possible equilibrium candidates. The strategy combination {*(defect, cooperate), cooperate*} is ruled out as an equilbrium by backwards induction.

---

11. All alternatives are summed in this manner. In this case, there are two alternative conditions for t, weak and strong.

Case (i): {cooperate, cooperate}. This equilibrium is determined (as are all of these equilibrium candidates) by Y's beliefs regarding X's type. This equilibrium occurs whenever Y's expected utility for cooperating exceeds that of defecting, such that $E_Y(cooperate) > E_Y(defect)$. This depends on Y's beliefs about X's type.

Case (ii): {cooperate, defect}. This equilibrium exists if Y's expected utility for defecting exceeds that of cooperating, such that $E_Y(cooperate) < E_Y(defect)$. This also depends on Y's beliefs.

Case (iii): {(defect, cooperate), defect}. This equilibrium exists when Y believes that X is weak, whereby: $E_Y(defect) < E_Y(cooperate)$.

Case (iv): (mixed strategy equilibrium). We can calculate the mixed strategy by estimating when the large power Y is indifferent between cooperating and defecting, such that $E_Y(cooperate) = E_Y(defect)$. To calculate Y's expected payoff from cooperating under conditions of incomplete information about X's type, we use Y's subjective beliefs about X's type, such that

$$E_Y(coop) = \mu_Y(t = strong|coop)4 + \mu_Y(t = weak|coop)2.$$

The expected payoffs for defecting are calculated similarly, such that

$$E_Y(defect) = \mu_Y(t = strong|coop)3 + \mu_Y(t = weak|coop)4.$$

Setting these equations equal to one another, we can calculate the portion of time Y would have to believe that X is strong for it to be indifferent between cooperating and defecting, such that

$$\mu_Y(t = strong|coop)4 + [1 - \mu_Y(t = strong|coop)]2$$
$$= \mu_Y(t = strong|coop)3 + [1 - \mu_Y(t = strong|coop)]4.$$

Simplifying this, we see

$$\mu_Y(t = strong|coop)2 + 2 = 4 - \mu_Y(t = strong|coop).$$

Further simplifying,

$$\mu_Y(t = strong|coop) = 2/3.$$

This means that Y's belief that given a decision by small power X to cooperate, it will face a strong X two-thirds of the time. In this manner we determine the mixed strategy equilibrium, where X has a weakly dominant strategy to cooperate and Y will cooperate or defect half of the time if it believes that X is strong two-thirds of the time.

This belief can also be used to determine the other equilibrium candidates. These results demonstrate a situation in which a large country's beliefs about the type of small country it faces can lead to cooperative behavior. We should note here that this result does not stem from the behavior of the small country X but from Nature and Y's beliefs about Nature's role in determining whether X is strong or weak. Beliefs and uncertainty play a big role in this game. Under certain conditions this uncertainty, coupled with the large power Y's beliefs about X, will lead it to cooperate. Such beliefs, in this way, lead to mutual cooperation. Accounting for the role of beliefs and incomplete information allows us to see how mutual cooperation could emerge between large and small trading partners.

Summary

In this chapter we have discussed the role of reputation, bluffing, and commitment. These three issues inherently involve situations in which one party lacks complete information about another. Beliefs play a big role in helping us analytically determine the equilibria for games with incomplete information. Backwards induction does not allow us to cross the multiple nodes that define games of incomplete information. By incorporating the concept of beliefs and utilizing Bayes' Theorem we can express the likelihood of a player's move from each node of an information set as an expected utility calculation. Beliefs determine the subjective probabilities of the expected utility calculation. Such a technique demonstrates how beliefs and strategies are interrelated.

By directly incorporating beliefs into our analysis we also can begin to explore the subjective aspects of choice and action. In the game theoretic models presented in this book, outcomes, actions, and choice stem from the interplay between beliefs and strategies. Equilibria derive directly from this interplay. To model the complexities of strategic political interaction realistically, we are sometimes going to have to incorporate beliefs into our analysis. Bluffing, reputation, and commitment play too big a role in politics to be ignored.

CHAPTER 7

Conclusion

Over the last 15 years the use of game theory in political science has exploded in popularity. Pick up any copy of the *American Political Science Review* or the *American Journal of Political Science* and this becomes quite evident. Yet, a good proportion of the political science community has no background or training in this methodology. We provide an introductory overview of game theoretic methodology in this book. However, our aim in writing this book is to address some common problems affecting a significant portion of work that applies game theory to political science. By attempting to clarify some popular misconceptions about game theoretic methodology and explicitly discussing what constitutes good work in this area, we hope to demonstrate the power and utility of game theoretic analysis.

In the introduction we discussed some basic principles that characterize good works in applied game theory. These criteria include: explicit assumptions, explicit and rigorous analysis (where the structure of the game is reproducible), and clear conclusions. The very best work also demands that we reassess the ways in which we view the world. Yet, despite the widespread use of some very sophisticated game theoretic techniques, there are many cases in which scholars fail to meet these criteria. All too often they rely heavily on extragame theoretic assumptions or analysis. Throughout this book we have focused on this problem. More specifically, we have identified some specific problems, including: not taking into account the strategic interaction between players, not explicitly modeling the structure of the game, and not explicitly modeling information asymmetries that may exist between political actors.

With these factors in mind, a summary of the chapters of the book is provided in the next section. This summary highlights the problems noted in the previous paragraph. Following this section, we provide the reader with a list of criteria for evaluating applications of game theory to political situations. This checklist reinforces the themes developed in this book.

Summary

Chapter 2 provided an overview of game theoretic techniques and a discussion of how to apply such models to politics. The chapter devotes considerable attention to the concepts of incomplete and imperfect information. Information asymmetries play an important role in political interactions. Game theoretic models provide a nice vehicle for explicitly accounting for the role information plays in politics. Using the example of the conflict between New Zealand and the United States, we demonstrate how to model political phenomena with game theory. In modeling this interaction, we illustrate how we can use different techniques to bring additional information into the model instead of relying on explanations outside of our game theoretic framework.

In chapters 3 and 4 we explored the differences between decision theory and game theory. When is a game really a game? Chapter 3 explicitly examines how the strategic interaction between political actors affects their behavior and compares this with situations in which there is no strategic interaction. In this chapter, we draw from Rohde (1979) to examine how using decision theory versus game theory alters our interpretation of a political phenomenon. Here we address a fundamental assumption of game theory. Does the political phenomenon in question involve strategic play between actors? Without strategic play, a decision theoretic framework is appropriate. With strategic play, one should turn to a game theoretic framework.

Chapter 4, in part, explores the same issue as chapter 3 does by contrasting two-player, small N-player, and large N-player games. Here we discuss how large numbers of players can fundamentally alter the nature of choice. The key difference is whether actors realize that their actions affect one another. The decisions made by actors in large N-player games are best modeled with decision theory; we see such situations in economics, where firms or consumers are price takers in a perfectly competitive market. When markets are not perfectly competitive and actors' decisions do affect one another, we should use game theoretic analysis. As with economics, political phenomena that involve large numbers of players, where individual actions do not affect others' behavior, should be modeled with decision theoretic models. Game theory should be employed when interactions are strategically motivated.

Chapter 4 also examines the importance of providing an explicit presentation and analysis of the structure of a game. By providing an explicit analysis of the structure of a game, some insights into the information conditions of the game can be obtained. Imperfect information, especially regarding the sequence of decisions that takes place in a game, can play a big role in some games. In particular, chapter 4 is an examination of Conybeare's analysis of trade conflict. We demonstrate how Conybeare's conclusions are strengthened by drawing exclusively on game theoretic analysis instead of factors outside his games.

Chapters 5 and 6 explore the issue of incomplete information, with particular emphasis on how players deal with uncertainty by updating their beliefs. Using the concept of perfect Bayesian equilibrium, we model this process. In chapter 5 we reexamine Przeworski's analysis of democratic transition. We show how explicitly modeling uncertainty enhances Przeworski's work. We are able to integrate the different models presented by Przeworski, deepening and strengthening his conclusions by only relying on game theoretic analysis.

Chapter 6 further examines specific topics of reputation, bluffs, commitment, and beliefs. Here we reanalyze some games presented in chapters 3 and 4, drawing on incomplete information and perfect Bayesian equilibrium. More specifically, we extend our analysis of progressive ambition among political candidates where politicians make their decisions under uncertainty about the electoral strength of the other candidate or possible candidate. We also extend our discussion of Conybeare's model of asymmetric trade with incomplete information. In addition, we consider efforts by one government to induce policy reform in another country (sometimes referred to as conditionality). By drawing on the perfect Bayesian equilibrium technique we are able to directly incorporate the issues of reputation, bluffs, and commitment to the updating of beliefs in these three examples.

In this book, our examples have been drawn from three subfields of political science. We used these cases to highlight the problems that need to be addressed when employing game theoretic methods. To a large extent we chose the three works by Rohde, Coneybeare, and Przeworski because of their widespread recognition. We do not mean specifically to call these works into question. In each case, our analysis never threatens the major thesis of the author; in fact, in most cases our analysis strengthens each author's claims. Instead, our focus is to model explicitly the assertions and contentions these authors make outside of their game theoretic framework. This problem is particularly relevant for Conybeare and Przeworski. We demonstrate here that game theoretic techniques can be applied to situations that integrate the authors' assertions. Using these techniques does not lead us to contradictory results; rather, the results strengthen Conybeare's and Przeworski's conclusions.

Applying Game Theoretic Models to Politics

In the previous section, we reviewed how we have dealt with integrating considerations that authors have left outside of their games into an explicit game theoretic framework. In this section, we provide readers with a checklist with which to consider their own applications of game theory to political interactions as well as those of others. When applying game theoretic methods to the analysis of politics, here are some specific points that should be addressed.

Assumptions
   —Have you made the assumptions clear?
   —Is the model consistent with the assumptions?
   —Have you identified all the actors that play the game?
   —Have you clearly explicated the characteristics of choice, information, and the game structure?
   —Have you been explicit about the payoffs?

Analysis
   —Have you been explicit about the actions, events, and general structure of the game?
   —Is the analysis of the equilibria explicit and clear? Is it replicable?
   —Have you been clear about what type of equilibrium conditions you have employed?

Conclusions
   —Are your conclusions clear?
   —Are your conclusions drawn from the analysis of your game? Do your conclusions stem from your equilibria analysis?
   —Have you been careful to employ assumptions and analysis that are related only to your game? Have you avoided drawing on nongame theoretic analysis?
   —If you alter your assumptions or analytical structure, how does this affect your game?
   —If you alter the equilibria concept, how does this affect the game?

After answering each of these, a final question should be addressed. This may be the most important of all: How does the game theoretic model help our understanding of politics?

Let us appraise each of the questions listed in the checklist. Start with the assumptions. Each of these questions is oriented toward getting you to think about making assumptions clear and formal. These questions also force you to think about which factors are to be considered explicitly within the game and which are not. One of game theory's chief advantages is the explicit nature of its assumptions. By being explicit about one's assumptions, one is able to be clear about which factors are important in the political interaction and which are not. Any analyst applying game theory to political science should be aware of this advantage and act accordingly.

Another advantage of game theory stems from the formal nature of the analysis employed. The questions asked concerning the analysis focus on such methodological issues as replicability and clarity of the analysis. At this stage, it is important to clearly note how the factors that you chose to include in the model through the selection of your assumptions fit into the game. In addition, it is also beneficial to think about how varying an analytical technique can lead to different conclusions. For example, do your results differ if you vary the amount of information that the various players possess, that is, changing a game of perfect information to one of imperfect information or changing a game of incomplete information to one of complete information? The more your results are reachable, regardless of these choices, the more robust your result will be.

The third advantage involves conclusions. Here the analyst is reminded of how the assumptions and analysis are interconnected and used to derive conclusions. These questions primarily deal with the sanctity of the model. Do your conclusions arise from your game theoretic approach or is your model discarded and replaced with extragame reasoning? Throughout this text, we have argued that many of the factors addressed through extragame factors can be integrated into the games themselves. It also important to note that in addition to outside factors we note the importance of examining the robustness of your results again. If you change your model slightly will you get different results? The more robust the model, the more confident we are of its results.

These three areas—assumptions, analysis, and conclusions—make game theoretic analysis a fruitful enterprise. The rigor and precision of this technique can lead us to startling new conclusions, call into question accepted perspectives, and provide a way of sifting through a complex and varied set of empirical analyses. All we need to do is let the method work for us, that is, apply it correctly and properly carry out application.

There are many advanced topics that we have not examined in this book. For the most part, the techniques we utilized are not sophisticated. Those looking for more technical and sophisticated modeling approaches should seek out a good text in game theory. We have limited our analysis to concepts that are more widely used and learned. Our chief aim is to demonstrate how game theoretic models can be used to effectively model political phenomena and conditions.

Game theoretic modeling techniques are available that can serve to strengthen work and, more importantly, to make such work analytically consistent. Game theory is a formal analytical tool that provides rigor and consistency to any analysis. Good game theory inherently involves the employment of explicit and clear analysis, rigorous analysis, and clear conclusions. Game theory benefits considerably from rigor and explicitness. That is what game theory is good for and how it should be used.

References

Abramson, Paul R., John H. Aldrich, and David W. Rohde. 1987. Progressive Ambition among United States Senators: 1972–1988. *Journal of Politics* 49:3–35.

Abramson, Paul R., John H. Aldrich, and David W. Rohde. 1995. *Change and Continuity in the 1994 Elections*. Washington, D.C.: Congressional Quarterly Press.

Aldrich, John H. 1993. Rational Choice and Turnout. *American Journal of Political Science* 37:246–78.

Aldrich, John. H., and William T. Bianco. 1991. A Game-Theoretic Model of Party Affiliation of Candidates and Office Holders. Unpublished Manuscript.

Aldrich, John H., and William T. Bianco. 1992. A Game-Theoretic Model of Party Affiliation of Candidates and Office Holders. *Mathematical and Computer Modelling* 16:103–16.

Alt, James, Randall L. Calvert, and Brian D. Humes. 1988. Reputation and Hegemonic Stability: A Game-theoretic Analysis. *American Political Science Review* 82:445–66.

Aumann, Robert J. 1989. Game Theory. In *The New Palgrave: Game Theory*, edited by John Eatwell, Murray Milgate, and Peter Newman. New York: W. W. Norton.

Aumann, Robert, ed. 1981. *Essays in Game Theory and Mathematical Economics in Honor of Oscar Morgenstern*. Mannheim: Bibliographisches Institut.

Austen-Smith, David. 1990. Information Transmission in Debate. *American Journal of Political Science* 34:120–52.

Austen-Smith, David, and Jeffrey S. Banks. 1989. Electoral Accountability and Incumbency. In *Models of Strategic Choice in Politics*, edited by Peter Ordeshook. Ann Arbor: University of Michigan Press.

Austen-Smith, David, and Jeffrey Banks. 1990. Stable Governments and the Allocation of Policy Portfolios. *American Political Science Review* 37:799–833.

Austen-Smith, David, and William H. Riker. 1987. Asymmetric Information and the Coherence of Legislation. *American Political Science Review* 81:897–918.

Austen-Smith, David, and William H. Riker. 1990. Asymmetric Information and the Coherence of Legislation: Correction. *American Political Science Review* 84:243–48.

Axelrod, Robert. 1970. *Conflict of Interest*. Chicago: Markham Press.

Axelrod, Robert. 1980a. Effective Choice in the Prisoners' Dilemma. *Journal of Conflict Resolution* 24:3–25.

169

Axelrod, Robert. 1980b. More Effective Choice in the Prisoners' Dilemma. *Journal of Conflict Resolution* 24:379–403.

Axelrod, Robert. 1981. The Emergence of Cooperation among Egoists. *American Political Science Review* 75:306–18.

Axelrod, Robert. 1984. *The Evolution of Cooperation*. New York: Basic Books.

Axelrod, Robert, and Lisa D'Ambrosia. 1994. Annotated Bibliography on *The Evolution of Cooperation*. Unpublished manuscript, University of Michigan.

Axelrod, Robert, and Doug Dion. 1988. The Further Evolution of Cooperation. *Science* 242:1385–90.

Axelrod, Robert, and Robert Keohane. 1985. Achieving Cooperation Under Anarchy: Strategies and Institutions. *World Politics* 38:226–54.

Bahnzhaf, J. 1965. Weighted Voting Doesn't Work: A Mathematical Study. *Rutgers Law Review* 19:317–43.

Banks, Jeffrey. 1989. Agency Budgets, Cost Information, and Auditing. *American Journal of Political Science* 33:670–99.

Banks, Jeffrey. 1991. *Signalling Games in Political Science*. New York: Harwood Academic Press.

Banks, Jeffrey S., and Roderick D. Kiewiet. 1989. Explaining Patterns of Candidate Competition in Congressional Elections. *American Journal of Political Science* 33:997–1015.

Banks, Jeffrey, and Joel Sobel. 1987. Equilibrium Selection in Signalling Games. *Econometrica* 55:647–61.

Banks, Jeffrey, and Barry Weingast. 1992. The Political Control of Bureaucracies under Asymmetric Information. *American Political Science Review* 36:509–25.

Baron, David. 1991. Majoritarian Incentives, Pork Barrel Programs, and Procedural Control. *American Journal of Political Science* 35:57–90.

Baron, David, and John Ferejohn. 1989. Bargaining in Legislatures. *American Political Science Review* 83:1181–206.

Bendor, Jonathan. 1988. Review Article: Formal Models of Bureaucracy. *British Journal of Political Science* 18:353–95.

Bendor, Jonathan, Serge Taylor, and Roland Van Gaalen. 1987. Politicians, Bureaucrats, and Asymmetric Information. *American Journal of Political Science* 31:796–828.

Bianco, William, and Robert Bates. 1990. Cooperation By Design: Leadership, Structure, and Collective Dilemmas. *American Political Science Review* 84:133–47.

Binmore, Ken. 1993. De-Bayesing Game Theory. In *Frontiers of Game Theory*, edited by Ken Binmore, Alan Kirman, and Piero Tani. Boston: MIT Press.

Brace, Paul. 1984. Progressive Ambition in the House: A Probabilistic Approach. *Journal of Politics* 46:556–71.

Brams, Steven J. 1978. *The Presidential Election Game*. New Haven: Yale University Press.

Brams, Steven J., and William H. Riker. 1972. Models of Coalition Formation in Voting Bodies. In *Mathematical Applications in Political Science, VI*, edited by J. L. Bernd. Charlottesville: University Press of Virginia.

Browne, Eric C. and Mark N. Franklin. 1973. Aspects of Coalition Payoffs in European Parliamentary Democracies. *American Political Science Review* 67:453–69.

Bueno de Mesquita, Bruce, and David Lalman. 1992. *War and Reason: Domestic and International Imperatives*. New Haven: Yale University Press.

Calvert, Randall. 1986. *Models of Imperfect Information in Politics*. New York: Harwood Academic Press.

Calvert, Randall. 1987. Reputation and Legislative Leadership. *Public Choice* 55:81–119.

Canon, David T., and David J. Sousa. 1992. Party System Change and Political Career Structures in the United States Congress. *Legislative Studies Quarterly* 17:347–63.

Cho, In-Koo, and David M. Kreps. 1987. Strategic Stability and Stable Equilibria. *Quarterly Journal of Economics* 102:179–221.

Conybeare, John A. C. 1987. *Trade Wars: The Theory and Practice of International Commercial Rivalry*. New York: Columbia University Press.

Copeland, Gary. 1989. Choosing to Run: Why House Members Seek Election to the Senate. *Legislative Studies Quarterly* 14:549–65.

Cox, Gary, and Mathew McCubbins. 1993. *Legislative Leviathan: Party Government in the House*. Berkeley: University of California Press.

Dekel, Eddie and Drew Fudenberg. 1990. Rational Play under Payoff Uncertainty. *Journal of Economic Theory* 52:243–67.

DeSwaan, Abraham. 1970. An Empirical Model of Coalition-formation as an *N*-person Game of Policy Distance Minimization. In *The Study of Coalition Behavior*, edited by Sven Groenning, E. Kelley, and Michael Leiserson. New York: Holt, Rinehart, and Winston.

Dodd, Lawrence. 1976. *Coalitions in Parliamentary Government*. Princeton: Princeton University Press.

Downs, George, and David M. Rocke. 1990. *Tacit Bargaining, Arms Races, and Arms Control*. Ann Arbor: University of Michigan Press.

Elster, Jon. 1984. *Ulysses and the Sirens: Studies in Rationality and Irrationality*. Rev. ed. New York: Cambridge University Press.

Enelow, James, and Melvin Hinich. 1984. *The Spatial Theory of Voting: An Introduction*. Cambridge: Cambridge University Press.

Fearon, James. 1990. Deterrence and the Spiral Model: The Role of Costly Signalling in Crisis Bargaining. Paper presented at the annual meetings of the American Political Science Association, San Francisco.

Fearon, James. 1994. Signalling versus the Balance of Power and Interests. *Journal of Conflict Resolution* 38:236–69.

Ferejohn, John. 1986. Logrolling in an Institutional Context: A Case Study of Food Stamp Legislation. In *Congress and Public Policy*, edited by Gerald C. Wright, Leroy N. Rieselbach, and Lawrence C. Dodd. New York: Agathon Press.

Fiorina, Morris. 1981. *Retrospective Voting in American National Elections*. New Haven: Yale University Press.

Fowler, Linda. 1993. *Candidates, Congress, and the American Democracy*. Ann Arbor: University of Michigan Press.

Friedman, James. 1971. A Noncooperative Equilibrium for Supergames. *Review of Economic Studies* 38: 1–12.

Friedman, James. 1986. *Game Theory with Applications to Economics*. New York: Oxford University Press.

Friedman, James. 1990. *Game Theory with Applications to Economics*. 2d ed. Boston: MIT Press.

Fudenberg, Drew, David Kreps, and David Levine. 1988. On the Robustness of Equilibrium Refinements. *Journal of Economic Theory* 44:354–80.

Fudenberg, Drew, and Eric Maskin. 1986. The Folk Theorem in Repeated Games with Discounting or with Incomplete Information. *Econometrica* 54:533–54.

Fudenberg, Drew, and Jean Tirole. 1991. *Game Theory*. Cambridge: MIT Press.

Gates, Scott. 1989. The Limits of Conditionality: An Examination of Individual Incentives and Structural Constraints. Ph.D. diss., University of Michigan.

Gates, Scott, and Sherry Bennett Quiñones. 1994. Game Theoretic and Empirical Methodologies: *Ever* the Two Shall Meet? *Political Methodologist* 6(2):30–36.

Geanakopolis, John. 1992. Common Knowledge. *Journal of Economic Perspectives* 6(4):58–82.

Geanakopolis, John. 1994. Common Knowledge. In *Handbook of Game Theory with Economic Applications*, Vol. 2, edited by Robert J. Aumann and Sergiu Hart. Amsterdam: North Holland Press.

Green, Donald, and Ian Shapiro. 1994. *Pathologies of Rational Choice Theory: A Critique and Applications in Political Science*. New Haven: Yale University Press.

Green, E., and R. Porter. 1984. Noncooperative Collusion Under Imperfect Price Information. *Econometrica* 52:87–100.

Harsanyi, John. 1967. Games of Incomplete Information Played by Bayesian Players. *Management Science* 14:159–82, 320–34, 486–502.

Hibbing, John R. 1982a. *Choosing to Leave*. Washington, D.C.: University Press of America.

Hibbing, John R. 1982b. Voluntary Retirement from the U.S. House: Who Quits? *American Journal of Political Science* 26:467–84.

Holmström, Bengt. 1982. Moral Hazard in Teams. *Bell Journal of Economics* 13(2):324–40.

Huth, Paul. 1988. *Extended Deterrence and the Prevention of War*. New Haven: Yale University Press.

Huth, Paul, and Bruce Russett. 1988. Deterrence Failure and Crisis Escalation. *International Studies Quarterly* 31:29–45.

Keohane, Robert. 1984. *After Hegemony: Cooperation and Discord in the World Political Economy*. Princeton: Princeton University Press.

Kiewiet, Rod, and Mathew McCubbins. 1991. *The Logic of Delegation: Congressional Parties and the Appropriations Process*. Chicago: University of Chicago Press.

Kilgour, D. Marc. 1991. Domestic Political Structure and War Behavior: A Game-Theoretical Approach. *Journal of Conflict Resolution* 35:266–84.

Kilgour, D. Marc., and Steven Brams. 1992. Putting the Other Side "on Notice" Can Induce Compliance in Arms Control. *Journal of Conflict Resolution* 36:395–414.

Kilgour, D. Marc., and Frank Zagare. 1991. Credibility, Uncertainty, and Deterrence. *American Journal of Political Science* 35:304–35.

King, Gary, Robert O. Keohane, and Sidney Verba. 1994. *Designing Social Inquiry. Scientific Inference in Qualitative Research*. Princeton: Princeton Univeristy Press.

Kohlberg, Elon, and Jean-Francois Mertens. 1986. On the Strategic Stability of Equilibria. *Econometrica* 54:1003–37.

Krehbiel, Keith. 1988. Spatial Models of Legislative Choice. *Legislative Studies Quarterly.* 8:259–319.

Krehbiel, Keith. 1991. *Information and Legislative Organization*. Ann Arbor: University of Michigan Press.

Kreps, David M. 1990. *A Course in Microeconomic Theory*. Princeton: Princeton University Press.

Kreps, David, and Robert Wilson. 1982. Reputation and Incomplete Information. *Journal of Economic Theory* 27:253–79.

Laver, Michael, and Kenneth Shepsle. 1990. Coalitions and Cabinet Government. *American Political Science Review* 84:873–90.

Laver, Michael and Kenneth Shepsle, eds. 1995. *Cabinet Ministers and Parliamentary Government*. Cambridge: Cambridge University Press.

Leiserson, Michael. 1968. Factions and Coalitions in One-party Japan: An Interpretation Based on the Theory of Games. *American Political Science Review* 62:770–87.

Lohmann, Susanne. 1993. Electoral Cycles and International Policy Cooperation. *European Economic Review* 37:1373–92.

Loomis, Burdette. 1984. Congressional Careers and Party Leadership in the Contemporary House. *American Journal of Political Science* 28:180–202.

Luce, R. Duncan, and Howard Raiffa. 1957. *Games and Decisions: Introduction and Critical Survey*. New York: John Wiley.

Lupia, Arthur. 1992. Busy Voters, Agenda Control, and the Power of Information. *American Political Science Review* 86:390–403.

Mann, Irwin, and Lloyd S. Shapley. 1964. "The *a priori* Voting Strength of the Electoral College. In *Game Theory and Related Approaches to Social Behavior*, edited by Martin Shubik. New York: Wiley.

Maynard-Smith, John. 1982. *Evolution and the Theory of Games*. Cambridge: Cambridge University Press.

McKelvey, Richard, and Peter Ordeshook. 1986. Elections with Limited Information: A Fulfilled Expectations Model Using Contemporaneous Poll and Endorsement Data as Information Sources. *Journal of Economic Theory* 36:55–85.

Milgrom, Paul, and John Roberts. 1982. Predation, Reputation, and Entry Deterrence. *Journal of Economic Theory* 27:280–312.

Miller, Gary J. 1992. *Managerial Dilemmas: The Political Economy of Hierarchy*. New York: Cambridge University Press.

Mo, Jongryn. 1994. Two-level Games with Endogenous Domestic Coalitions. *Journal of Conflict Resolution* 38:402–22.

Morrow, James D. 1989. Capabilities, Uncertainty, and Resolve: A Limited Information Model of Crisis Bargaining. *American Journal of Political Science* 33:941–72.

Morrow, James D. 1994. *Game Theory for Political Scientists*. Princeton: Princeton University Press.

Morton, Rebecca. 1993. Incomplete Information and Ideological Explanations of Platform Divergence. *American Political Science Review* 87:382–92.

Moulin, Hervé. 1986. *Game Theory for the Social Sciences*. 2d ed. New York: New York University Press.

Myerson, Roger. 1991. *Game Theory: Analysis of Conflict*. Cambridge: Harvard University Press.

Myerson, Roger. 1992. On the Value of Game Theory in Social Sciences. *Rationality and Society* 4:62–73.

Myerson, Roger, and Robert Weber. 1993. A Theory of Voting Equilibria. *American Political Science Review* 87:102–14.

Nalebuff, Barry. 1986. Brinksmanship and Nuclear Deterrence: The Neutrality of Escalation. *Conflict Management and Peace Science* 9:19–30.

Nash, John F. 1950. Eqlubrium Points in *N*-person Games. *Proceedings of the National Academy of Science* 36:48–49.

Nash, John F. 1951. Non-cooperative Games. *Annals of Mathematics* 54:286–95.

Niou, Emerson M. S., and Peter J. Ordeshook. 1990. Stability in Anarchic International Systems. *American Political Science Review* 84:1207–34.

O'Neill, Barry. 1994. Game Theory Models of Peace and War. In *Handbook of Game Theory With Economic Applications,* Vol. 2, edited by Robert J. Aumann and Sergiu Hart. Amsterdam: North Holland Press.

Ordeshook, Peter C. 1986. *Game Theory and Political Theory.* Cambridge: Cambridge University Press.

Ordeshook, Peter C. 1992. *A Political Theory Primer.* New York: Routledge.

Ordeshook, Peter and Emerson Niou. 1989a. The Geographical Imperatives of the Balance of Power in Three-country Systems. *Mathematics and Computer Modelling* 12:519–31.

Ordeshook, Peter, and Emerson Niou. 1989b. Stability in International Systems and the Costs of War. In *Models of Strategic Choice in Politics,* edited by Peter Ordeshook. Ann Arbor: University of Michigan Press.

Ordeshook, Peter, and William H. Riker. 1973. *An Introduction to Positive Political Theory.* Englewood Cliffs, N.J.: Prentice Hall.

Oye, Kenneth A., ed., 1986. *Cooperation under Anarchy.* Princeton: Princeton University Press.

Palfrey, Thomas, ed. 1991. *Laboratory Research in Political Science.* Ann Arbor: University of Michigan Press.

Palfrey, Thomas, and Howard Rosenthal. 1985. Voter Participation and Strategic Uncertainty. *American Political Science Review* 79:62–78.

Poundstone, William. 1992. *Prisoners' Dilemma: John von Neumann, Game Theory, and the Puzzle of the Bomb.* New York: Doubleday.

Powell, Robert. 1988. Nuclear Brinkmanship with Two-sided Incomplete Information. *American Political Science Review* 82:155–78.

Powell, Robert. 1990. *Nuclear Deterrence Theory: The Search for Credibility.* Cambridge: Cambridge University Press.

Przeworski, Adam. 1991. *Democracy and the Market: Political and Economic Reforms in Eastern Europe and Latin America.* Cambridge: Cambridge University Press.

Quine, William V. 1953. Two Dogmas of Empiricism. *From a Logical Point of View.* Cambridge: Harvard University Press.

Quiñones, Sherry Bennett. 1992. International Coordination of Macroeconomic Policy: The Role of Leadership and Triggering Strategies in a Cooperative Policy Regime. Paper presented at the annual meeting of the Midwest International Studies Association, Michigan State University, East Lansing, November 20.

Quiñones, Sherry Bennett, and Scott Gates. 1993. International Trade Policy Coordination: Controlling Moral Hazard Problems with Regime Leadership.

Paper presented at the University of Illinois, Merriam Laboratory, Champaign-Urbana, October.

Rappoport, Anatol, and Albert Chammah. 1965. *Prisoners' Dilemma: A Study in Conflict and Cooperation.* Ann Arbor: University of Michigan Press.

Rasmussen, Eric. 1989. *Games and Information.* Cambridge: Basil Blackwell.

Riker, William H. 1963. *Theory of Political Coalitions.* New Haven: Yale University Press.

Riker, William H. 1990."Political Science and Rational Choice. In *Perspectives of Positive Political Economy*, edited by James E. Alt and Kenneth A. Shepsle. Cambridge: Cambridge University Press.

Riker, William H., and Lloyd S. Shapley. 1968. Weighted Voting: A Mathematical Analysis for Instrumental Judgements. In *Representation*, edited by J. R. Pennock and J. W. Chapman. New York: Atherton.

Robeck, Bruce. 1982. State Legislator Candidacies for the United States House: Prospects for Success. *Legislative Studies Quarterly* 7:507–14.

Rohde, David W. 1979. Risk-bearing and Progressive Ambition: The Case of Members of the United States House of Representatives. *American Journal of Political Science* 23:1–26.

Sapiro, Virginia. 1982. Private Costs of Public Commitments or Public Costs of Private Commitments? Family Roles versus Political Ambition. *American Journal of Political Science* 26:265–79.

Schelling, Thomas. 1980. The Intimate Contest for Self-Control. *The Public Interest* 60:94–118.

Schlesinger, Joseph. 1966. *Ambition and Politics: Political Careers in the United States.* Chicago: Rand McNally.

Schofield, Norman, and Michael Laver. 1985. Bargaining Theory and Portfolio Payoffs in European Coalition Governments, 1945–1983. *British Journal of Political Science* 15:143–64.

Selten, Reinhart. 1965. Spieltheoretische Behandlung eines Oligopolmodells mit Nachfragetragheit. *Zeitschrift für die gesammte Staatswissenschaft* 121:301–24, 667–89.

Selten, Reinhart. 1975. Reexamination of the Perfectness Concept for Equilibrium Points in Extensive Games. *International Journal of Game Theory* 4:25–55.

Selten, Reinhart. 1978. The Chain-Store Paradox. *Theory and Decision* 9:127–59.

Shapley, Lloyd S., and Martin Shubik. 1954. A Method of Evaluating the Distribution of Power in a Committee System. *American Political Science Review* 48:787–92.

Shepsle, Kenneth. 1979. Institutional Arrangements and Equilibrium in Multidimensional Voting Models. *American Journal of Political Science* 23:27–59.

Shepsle, Kenneth. 1991. *Models of Multiparty Competition.* New York: Harwood Academic Press.

Shepsle, Kenneth, and Barry Weingast. 1987. The Institutional Foundation of Committee Power. *American Political Science Review* 81:85–104.

Shepsle, Kenneth A., and Barry R. Weingast. 1995. *Positive Theories of Congressional Institutions.* Ann Arbor: University of Michigan Press.

Shubik, Martin. 1970. Game Theory, Behavior and the Paradox of the Prisoners' Dilemma: Three Solutions. *Journal of Conflict Resolution*, 14:181–93.

Shubik, Martin. 1982. *Game Theory in the Social Sciences: Concepts and Solutions*. Cambridge: MIT Press.

Snidal, Duncan. 1985. The Game Theory of International Relations. *World Politics* 38:25–57.

Squire, Peverill. 1989. Competition and Uncontested Seats in United States House Elections. *Legislative Studies Quarterly* 14:281–95.

Squire, Peverill. 1991. Preemptive Fundraising and Challenger Profiles in Senate Elections. *Journal of Politics* 53:1150–64.

Straffin, Philip D. 1977. Homogeneity, Independence, and Power Indices. *Public Choice* 30:107–18.

Taylor, Michael. 1976. *Anarchy and Cooperation*. New York: John Wiley & Sons.

Taylor, Michael. 1987. *The Possiblity of Cooperation*. New York: Cambridge University Press.

Taylor, Michael, and Michael Laver. 1973. Government Coalitions in Western Europe. *European Journal of Political Science* 1:205–48.

Tirole, Jean. 1988. *The Theory of Industrial Organization*. Boston: MIT Press.

Trockel, Walter. 1986. The Chain-Store Paradox Revisited. *Theory and Decision*. 21:163–79.

von Neumann, John. 1928. Zur Theorie de Gesellschaftsspiele. *Mathematische Annalen* 100:295–320.

von Neumann, John, and Oskar Morgenstern. 1944. *Theory of Games and Economic Behavior*. Princeton: Princeton Univeristy Press.

Wagner, Harrison R. 1983. The Theory of Games and the Problem of International Cooperation. *American Political Science Review* 77:330–46.

Wagner, Harrison. 1991. Nuclear Deterrence, Counterforce Strategies, and the Incentive to Strike First. *American Political Science Review* 85:727–49.

Weingast, Barry. 1989. Floor Behavior in the U.S. Congress: Committee Power under the Open Rule. *American Political Science Review* 83:795–815.

Wittman, Donald. 1989. Arms Control Verification and Other Games Involving Imperfect Detection. *American Political Science Review* 89:923–48.

Yarbrough, Beth V., and Robert M. Yarbrough. 1985. Free Trade, Hegemony, and the Theory of Agency. *Kyklos* 38:348–64.

Yarbrough, Beth V., and Robert M. Yarbrough. 1986. Reciprocity, Bilateralism, and Economic Hostages. *International Studies Quarterly* 30:7–22.

Index

namic games; Finitely repeated play; Infinitely repeated games

Reputation, 5, 20, 56, 107, 114, 124, 136–39, 141–61, 165. *See also* Beliefs; Perfect Bayesian equilibrium; Repeated games, of incomplete information

Riker, William, 2, 3, 13, 14

Risk, 64, 69, 71, 73

Roberts, John, 142, 143

Rocke, David, 5

Rohde, David, 13, 19, 67–81, 141, 157, 164, 165

Rosenthal, Howard, 5

Russett, Bruce, 16

Sanction game, 147–53. *See also* Conditionality game

Schlesinger, Joseph, 69

Schofield, Norman, 3

Selten, Reinhart, 4, 92, 141–43, 145

Sequential games: in extensive form, 40–42, 96–102; in matrix form, 36–39, 99–100. *See also* Dynamic games; Extensive form games; Games, of complete and perfect information; Stackelberg games

Sequential equilibrium, 4, 17, 146. *See also* Equilibrium; Incomplete information; Perfect Bayesian equilibrium; Subgame perfect equilibrium

Shapiro, Ian, 10

Shapley, Lloyd, 2, 3

Shepsle, Kenneth, 13

Shubik, Martin, 2, 57, 95

Signaling, 5, 13. *See also* Commitment; Reputation

Solution concepts, 12

Stackelberg games, 96–102. *See also* Extensive form games; Sequential games; Stackelberg equilibria

Stackelberg equilibria, 98–100. *See also* Subgame perfect equilibria

Stag Hunt, 33, 85, 96, 100, 157. *See also* Hybrid Chicken–Stag Hunt; Matrix form games; Two by two games

Strategic interaction, 1, 7, 9, 19, 61, 74, 83, 84, 103, 113, 136, 166–67

Strategy, 3, 12, 85, 87

Structure, of a game, 6, 7, 23–25; of an extensive form game, 40

Subgame perfect equilibrium, 4, 19, 42, 44, 93, 97, 98–100, 106, 135, 142. *See also* Equilibrium; Nash equilibrium; Perfect Bayesian equilibrium; Stackelberg equilibria

Subjective probability, 79, 122. *See also* Beliefs; Expected values

Symmetric game, 30, 79

Taylor, Michael, 3, 5

Taylor, Serge, 5

Threat, 92, 110

Transitivity, 8, 9. *See also* Game Theory, assumptions; Rational choice

Trigger strategy, 106, 109–11; grim trigger (*g*-trigger), 108; leader trigger (*l*-trigger), 110; strategic trigger (*s*-trigger), 109. *See also* *N*-player games

Trockel, Walter, 145, 150

Two by two games, 33. *See also* Asymmetric trade game; Chicken; Deadlock; Hybrid Chicken–Stag Hunt; Prisoners' dilemma; Stag Hunt

Two-sided incomplete information, 134–36. *See also* Asymmetric information; Incomplete information

Uncertainty, 4, 113, 118, 122, 124–25, 130, 134–35, 144–46. *See also* Certainty; Incomplete information

Utility: and decision theory, 63–64; and preferences, 9. *See also* Expected utility

United States, 23, 30–59

Van Gaalen, Ronald, 5

Verba, Sydney, 6

von Neumann, John, 1–3, 103